CREATIVE CHILDREN, IMAGINATIVE TEACHING

Florence Beetlestone

Open University Press
Buckingham · Philadelphia

Open University Press
Celtic Court
22 Ballmoor
Buckingham
MK18 1XW

email: enquiries@openup.co.uk
world wide web: http://www.openup.co.uk

and
325 Chestnut Street
Philadelphia, PA 19106, USA

First Published 1998

A catalogue record of this book is available from the British Library

ISBN   0 335 19783 (pb)   0 335 19784 1 (hb)

Library of Congress Cataloging-in-Publication Data
Beetlestone, Florence, 1943–
    Creative children, imaginative teaching / Florence Beetlestone.
      p. cm. – (Enriching the primary curriculum–child, teacher,
    context)
    Includes bibliographical references and index.
    ISBN 0-335-19784-1. – ISBN 0-335-19783-3 (pbk.)
    1. Creative thinking in children–Great Britain. 2. Learning, Psy-
chology of. 3. Creative activities and seat work–Great Britain.
4. Curriculum planning–Great Britain. 5. Elementary school teaching–Great Britain. I. Title. II. Series.
LB1062.B43 1998
370.15'7–dc21   97-31568
                                             CIP

Copy-edited and typeset by The Running Head Limited, London and
    Cambridge

Printed and bound in Great Britain by
Marston Book Services Limited, Oxford

CREATIVE CHILDREN,
IMAGINATIVE TEACHING

Enriching the primary curriculum: child, teacher, context

Series editor: Janet Moyles

This series highlights some of the major challenges and issues which face teachers on a day-to-day basis in handling their apparently ever widening roles in primary schools. Curriculum experiences can, and should be enriching and stimulating for everyone but there must be a recognition and appreciation of the crucial interface between child, teacher and the context of school and society, rather than a focus on mere curriculum 'delivery'.

Each volume in the series seeks to enrich and extend readers' curriculum thinking beyond the current narrow confines through recognizing and celebrating the very essence of what makes primary teaching demanding but exciting, creative, dynamic and, yes, even enjoyable! The series recognizes that at the heart of teaching lies children and that 'subjects' are merely tools towards enabling an education which develops both understanding and enthusiasm for life-long learning.

The authors' underpinning, integrated rationale is to enable teachers to analyse their own practices by exploring those of others through cameos of real life events taken from classroom and school contexts. The aim throughout is to help teachers regain their sense of ownership over changes to classroom and curricular practices and to develop an enhanced and enriched understanding of theory through practice.

Current and forthcoming titles:

To Liz and Jon

Contents

Series editor's preface

Cameo

Glenn has taught across the age range in different primary schools for the last 15 years, specializing in art. In that time, he has had to make many adjustments in his thinking. The emphasis now appears to have shifted significantly from considering the learning needs of children as paramount, to 'delivering' a curriculum over which he feels little ownership and about which he feels even less real enthusiasm! The National Curriculum, with its individual subjects and language of 'teaching', not to mention an impending Office for Standards in Education (Ofsted) inspection, has shaken his confidence somewhat in his own understanding of what primary education is all about. It has also meant that he feels *he* is doing most of the learning, rather than the children – all those detailed plans and topic packs for individual subjects which teachers have been developing within the school seem to Glenn to leave little for children to actually do except explore the occasional artefact and fill in worksheets.

Yet he knows that he enjoys the 'buzz' of teaching, revels in being part of children's progress and achievements, delights in those rare times when he can indulge in art activities with children, is appreciated by parents and colleagues for the quality of his work and, generally, still finds his real heart lies in being an educator and doing something worthwhile. His constant question to himself is 'How can I work with children in ways I feel and *know* are appropriate and yet meet the outside demands made on me?'

Sound familiar? You may well begin to recognize a 'Glenn' within you! He encapsulates the way many teachers are feeling at the present time and the persistent doubts and uncertainties which continually underpin many teachers' work. In the early and middle years of primary schooling in particular, teachers are facing great challenges in conceiving how best to accommodate the learning needs of children in a context of growing pressure, innovation and subject curriculum demand. Yet conscientiousness drives the professional to strive for greater understanding – that little bit more knowledge or skill might just make a big difference to one child, or it might provide improved insights into one aspect of the curriculum.

Glenn, like many teachers, needs time, encouragement and support to reflect on his current practice and to consider in an objective way the changes needed. Rather than trying to add something else to an already overcrowded curriculum, today's teachers should consider those existing aspects which are fundamental to ensuring that children are not only schooled but educated in the broadest possible sense. Only then can we begin to sort out those things which are vital, those things we would like to do, and those things which would benefit from a rethink.

This series aims to offer practitioners food for thought as well as practical and theoretical support in establishing, defining and refining their own understandings and beliefs. It focuses particularly on enriching curriculum experiences for everyone through recognizing and appreciating the crucial interface between the child, the teacher and the context of primary education, including the curriculum context. Each title in the series seeks collectively and individually to enhance teachers' understanding about the theories which underpin, guide and enrich quality practice in a range of broader curriculum aspects, while acknowledging issues such as class size and overload, common across primary schools today.

Each book operates from the basis of exploring teachers' sound – frequently intuitive – experiences and understanding of teaching and learning processes and outcomes which most teachers inevitably possess in good measure and which, like Glenn, they often feel constrained to use. For example, the editor is regularly told by teachers and others in primary schools that they 'know' or 'feel' that play for children is or must be a valuable process, yet they are also aware that this is not often reflected in their planning or curriculum management and that the context of education generally is antithetical to play. What is more, they really do not know what to do about it and find articulating the justification for play practices extremely difficult. Other writers in the series have suggested that this is also the case in their areas of expertise.

All the books in this series seek to enrich and extend teachers' curriculum thinking beyond the level of just 'subjects', into dimensions related to the teaching and learning needs of children and the contextual demands faced by schools. The books cover areas such as creativity, success and competence, exploration and problem solving, information technology across subjects and boundaries, play in the primary curriculum, questioning and teacher–child interactions, values in relation to equality issues, social, moral and spiritual frameworks, and physical aspects of teaching and learning. Each book has had, within its working title, the rationale of the unique triad of child, teacher and context which underpins all primary schooling and education, for example in this particular case, creative children and imaginative teaching. This structure serves to emphasize for authors the inextricable and imperative balance in this triad for effective classroom and curriculum practices. The model we have developed and agreed is shown in Figure 1.

All the writers in the series have been concerned to emphasize the quality, nature and extent of existing classroom practices, and how it is possible to build on these sound pedagogical bases. For

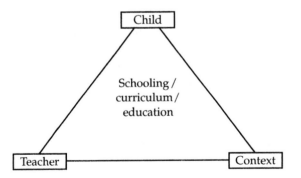

Figure 1 Child, teacher, context

this reason, chapters within each title often begin with two or more cameos offering features of practice as starting points for teasing out aspects requiring enquiry, analysis, evaluation and discussion. Chapters then develop their own relevant themes but with consistent reference to what these mean to children and teachers within the general autonomy, and constraints, of the school context.

Issues concerning the *child* take their stance from cognitive psychology (as this book does) and include the child as:

- an active searcher after meaning;
- an individual with particular perceptions of the world and their part in it;
- a person who can reflect on their own learning and understanding;
- a learner with his or her own curriculum needs and interests to be considered;
- an interactive person, learning in collaboration with peers and adults;
- a unique individual but also one with collective needs;
- a member of a 'social' community, i.e. home, family, school, wider community.

Aspects to do with the teaching role lay stress on the *teacher* as a reflective and critical professional who will occasionally but regularly need to stand back from day-to-day practice in order to think about and analyse the triadic relationships and to acknowledge:

- their own learning styles and experiences;
- their own beliefs, values, knowledge and conceptual understanding of pedagogy;
- their need to raise questions about practice and find solutions in an ongoing way;
- their role as mutual learners with children and colleagues;
- their responsibilities as facilitators of learning, as models of learning and as negotiators of meaning with children;
- their role in enabling children's learning rather than always in 'teaching';
- their function as observers and assessors of children's understandings as well as outcomes;
- their obligation clearly to conceptualize the whole curriculum of which the National Curriculum is a part.

When we consider the *context* of pedagogy, this focus subsumes such aspects as the learning environment, school ethos and the actual classroom and school. It also includes such elements as:

- the physical environment – indoors and outdoors;
- the social environment of school and schooling (e.g. is the child an outcome of the context or has the context influenced the child?);
- the psychological environment of school and schooling;
- the philosophical considerations within schools and aspects such as teachers' beliefs and values;
- the curriculum context, including the National Curriculum where this is relevant and appropriate, but also showing where this does not necessarily meet pedagogical needs;
- the frameworks within which the whole concept of schooling takes place and where this fits education in a broader sense.

The overall rationale for each book in the series starts from a belief that teachers should be enabled to analyse their own practices in specific aspects of the broader curriculum as a major aspect of their professionalism. The books are particularly useful at a time of continual curriculum change, when reflection is being focused back upon the child and pedagogy generally as the only perpetuating and consistent elements.

As an integral component, all the books weave teachers' assessment of children's learning and understanding into each particular focus, the intention being to show how the planning> learning>assessment>planning cycle is vital to the quality and success of children's and teachers' learning experiences. With their practical ideas, challenges and direct relevance to classroom practice, these books offer ways of establishing theory as *the* adjunct to practice; they build on teachers' thinking about how they already work in the classroom and help teachers to consider how they may enrich, extend and advance their practices to the mutual benefit of themselves, the children, the curriculum and education in society as a whole.

Creative Children, Imaginative Teaching covers a key aspect of teaching and learning which is vital yet often uninvestigated because of its complexity. In a lively and accessible account, Florence Beetlestone explores the various and heterogeneous strands which constitute the concept of creativity in the context of pedagogy, exhorting practitioners to consider creativity far beyond the realms of 'art', with which it is frequently associated. She points out that looking at creativity only in the context of subject curriculum narrows what is potentially a wide ranging approach: broadening the definition can make learning more meaningful and enjoyable, teaching more stimulating and imaginative, and the curriculum broader and more exciting.

Do all children and teachers have the potential to be creative? Can basic numeracy and literacy skills be readily incorporated into creative activities? Are creative people necessarily non-conformist? What are the links between creative thinking and problem solving? These and many other questions are probed throughout this book. It offers a significant contribution to our understanding of the ways in which being creative and imaginative can act as a catalyst for curriculum implementation, management and development. Many teachers express the view that creativity is an underestimated and undervalued aspect of schooling; they will welcome the book's support for promoting this essential aspect of children's education. Florence takes current ideas from a range of sources and brings them together to make a persuasive case which teachers can use to promote and extend creativity in early years and primary schooling.

The cameos presented offer a wide variety of considered examples of classroom contexts. Florence then teases out aspects to provoke readers' own thinking on the issues; she also provides sound ideas for extending and enriching their practices. Readers will quickly recognize Florence's own commitment to, and originality of ideas for, engaging children in creative processes and outcomes. Issues related to assessment of achievement and understanding also feature strongly as elements of learning, as do the implications of creative approaches for the teacher's role. Ways of counteracting some of the inevitable constraints to creativity and originality within some contexts are openly and thoughtfully examined, and ways forward – creative ones, of course – are explored. Practical ideas supported with strong theoretical underpinnings are presented to show how creative approaches can be adopted by busy primary teachers to enrich the curriculum provision they make for young learners, as well as to fulfil external and school demands. Each chapter will challenge teachers to reflect on their practice and, hopefully, re-evaluate their stance on what it is to be 'creative' in the context of quality education.

To 'create', according to the Oxford Dictionary, is to 'bring into existence'. Those of you who desire to enrich the curriculum for the children you teach will be glad that this book exists within the series. It is a powerful advocate for the importance of developing your own imaginative teaching and ensuring that there are creative children for the new millennium.

Janet Moyles

Acknowledgements

I am particularly indebted to my own children, my nephews David and Andrew, and to the many children I have taught at the Claremont Pre-School Playgroup, Broadwater Farm Nursery, Devonshire Hill Primary and Culloden Primary. I owe a debt to all the children, parents, teachers and head teachers I have worked with over the years and who have collectively given me insight, understanding and a bank of experience and examples to draw upon. There have been many creative individuals among them.

My students at the University of Greenwich, whether on BEd, PGCE or inservice programmes, have clarified my vision of what quality teaching is all about: in exploring the complexities of teaching and learning with them, I have come to understand the processes more fully. I thank them for their energy, enthusiasm and commitment.

Thanks must also be expressed to colleagues at Avery Hill, particularly those in the Early Years Team, who have always been personally very supportive and encouraging. I also owe a debt of gratitude to the educational authorities which have provided the creative framework for the schools in which I have worked, particularly the London Boroughs of Enfield, Haringey, Tower Hamlets and Greenwich, and those in Sweden and Norway.

I would also like to thank the series editor, Janet Moyles, who has supported and encouraged my work throughout the writing of this book, and Shona Mullen, who has carefully and thoughtfully guided its production from the early stages.

It is difficult to single out individuals, but special thanks are due to three teachers who have provided me with role models for this book: Fiona Cribb, Julia Thorne and Lesley Neville, together with their head teachers, Gillean Paterson, Anna Coote and Dave Suttle, who provided the supportive school settings which enabled these teachers to be truly creative. In Lesley's class in particular, I found a complete example of creative children, a creative teacher and a creative context.

Introduction

> Education must demonstrate how creative energy and inventiveness have constantly improved the context, content and quality of human life.
>
> (Norwegian National Curriculum, in Hagness 1994: 11)

How wonderful it is to see creativity placed so firmly at the centre of the Norwegian curriculum. In the UK it is not so central; indeed, it would appear that creativity has very much taken a 'back seat' since the advent of the National Curriculum, arguably because it is so much more difficult to deliver and assess than subject content. However, a lot can be gained by looking at creativity and the way it is developed in schools: we can begin to question our system and its policies and practices, take on new perspectives and re-examine our values. This is particularly important in the early and primary years when the foundations for learning are established and the patterns for future development laid down. Teaching creatively can improve the quality of education, make learning more meaningful and open up more exciting ways of approaching the curriculum.

Not everyone, of course, has the same definition of creativity. As a broad and somewhat abstract concept it is bound to lead to a number of interpretations. There are 'relevant criteria but no definitive criteria' (Fryer 1996: 26). The definition used in this book is my particular construct which subsumes many of the elements embodied in other definitions and which I have used to define creativity in relation to the teaching of young children.

My construct has six key strands:

- creativity as a form of learning;
- representation;
- productivity;
- originality;
- thinking creatively/problem solving;
- universe/creation-nature.

Creativity as a form of learning

This is a vital part of cognitive functioning (Gardner 1993). It can help to explain and interpret abstract concepts by involving skills such as curiosity, inventiveness, exploration, wonder and enthusiasm, which are all qualities young children have in abundance. These aspects can be harnessed by giving children greater technical mastery and wider vision so that creativity can inform all other learning.

Representation

Creativity involves expressing ideas and feelings and using a range of ways to do so, for example through the expressive arts. This is the way creativity is popularly perceived and, as Fryer (1996: 123) points out, the way most teachers learnt it at colleges. Creativity thus covers the elements of symbolism, role play, acting, drawing, graphics, illustration, painting, producing a likeness, tracing, printing, engraving, sculpture, art, fine art, photography, map making, imitation and description. This strand of creativity is often seen as therapeutic, since it allows individuals to respond emotionally and to express their inner feelings about the world around them: a spiritual reflection on the world they perceive. The idea of self-expression is central to this strand, as in a healthy emotional state the subconscious needs to be expressed rather than suppressed (Egan and Nadaner 1988: xi). The expressive arts provide a particularly important way of doing this.

Productivity

Creativity involves making: using the imagination, creating, composing, authorship, musical skill, performance, planning, constructing, building, technological skills and large and small scale output – it is almost like a production line. Integral to the process of creation is destruction, the 'negative as well as the positive' (Fryer 1996: 62); old ideas may need to be demolished before new ones can be put into place.

Originality

This is the strand of creativity concerned with making unusual connections, Mednick's 'remote, previously unassociated ideas' (Fryer 1996: 47): the transfer of specialist knowledge from one area to another, inventiveness, imagination, prototypes, specialness, newness, freshness, individuality, non-conformity, difference, independence, inimitability, the ability to be out of the ordinary, unexpected and to take risks.

Thinking creatively/problem solving

This aspect of creativity takes it beyond the expressive arts to cover all walks of life. The creative process involves selecting elements known from various quarters and amalgamating them into new formats; using information in new situations; drawing on disconnected aspects of experience, patterns, analogies and underlying principles. These aspects enable the problem solver to come up with different and less obvious solutions. Creative problem solving can be developed extensively in science, maths and business, for example, and is a quality that is much needed in today's economic climate. A good summary of some of the creative development programmes used to extend thinking can be found in Fryer (1996: 90–8). Thinking creatively does not imply that creative thinking is qualitatively different; what I mean by the term is the reflective process referred to in Figure 5.4 which is an integral part of the creative process. Problem solving enables us to adopt creative behaviour, 'an exaggerated push for change' (Parnes 1985: 4), and is therefore an important part of creative teaching.

Universe/creation-nature

This is the strand of creativity which is linked to the source of creation, inspiration, mood, source of creative drive, energy, awe, wonder, appreciation of beauty, awareness of natural order, pro-creation, the cycle of growth and death, growing, farming, living things. The creative process thus involves an emotional interaction between the individual and the environment. The environment will be interpreted by individuals according to their emotional response. If human consciousness and the human mind can be seen to have either 'impressions' or 'ideas' (Warnock 1976: 14), all experiences can be divided between what is fact (ideas) and the 'sensations, passions and emotions' (impressions) by which we interpret them. All our views of the world are, therefore, bound by definition to be subjective and coloured by our response to nature as a whole.

Overall the strands of my construct of creativity bind together elements from philosophical, spiritual, psychological and socio-logical perspectives. These strands form the basis of each chapter; they also weave their way in and out of different chapters. My intention throughout is to link these effectively to the framework of the National Curriculum and to show ways of increasing creativity within it. The strands are set in a learning framework which draws on much pre-National Curriculum thinking. My understanding of children's learning and developmentally appropriate forms of practice stems from the nursery/infant school traditions based on the work of those referred to by Bruce (1987: 9) as the 'pioneers': Froebel, Montessori and Steiner (see also Gammage and Meighan 1993). The ideas of Bruner, Vygotsky and Piaget permeate our understanding (see Merry 1997) and under-lie the approach used in this book. In addition, much work on creativity was conducted in the 1960s, which was a period of great interest in harnessing creative potential. There have been few subsequent in-depth studies, and so I have been influenced in my thinking by the work of Hudson, Guilford, McKinnon and Torrance from that period.

What then do we mean by creative teaching? Let's look at two examples, both with Year 2 classes.

In classroom A the teacher has decided to have a 'creative' Friday afternoon. The session is not formally planned; instead she tells the children to make a model of their favourite room and to decorate it. They can use any of the materials – junk, plasticine, paints, crayons, felt tips – and make their model in any way they like. The children proceed busily at first, but show little inclination to plan or to think through ideas. Materials are selected and used without care so that there is a lot of waste and mess. Several children laugh at the efforts of one child and the teacher does not intervene. Nor does she notice that several children have good ideas which they are unable to put into practice. One does ask for help, but is told to 'think of your own ideas'.

Class B has also been told to 'be creative'. However they have been given a clear brief. They are designing a town garden. The teacher has a good knowledge of the subject, the class have been to look at several local gardens and they have looked at a range of books on the subject in the previous week. The children have been given an idea of size and scale, given pencils and sketching paper. They have been told to think of as many ideas as possible and to try them out with various sketches until they find an idea they are happy with. The children have scope to be creative and imaginative, their ideas channelled by a clear task and by the appropriate materials. As they are working the teacher wanders round discussing each child's ideas, listening, supporting and guiding. By careful questions she is able to get children to extend their ideas and to think through the practicalities of their designs. It is clear to all that everyone's ideas are valued and that it is unusual ideas that can be particularly interesting. No child feels discouraged and the teacher is able to see where real effort needs further encouragement.

The first example illustrates the sort of 'creative' activity which is all too often seen in primary schools. It is unplanned, has little teacher input or direction and shows scant regard for selection of materials or fitting them to the task. This kind of session can result in mess, wastage and questionable learning experiences for children, who can be easily discouraged because their efforts are not valued by their peers and teaching is minimal.

The model of creative teaching which forms the basis for this book is quite different; in fact, it is the opposite of this laissez faire approach. Many of the characteristics of creative teaching are similar to those mentioned by Fryer (1996: 75). Like the teacher in example B, the creative teacher demonstrates:

- commitment;
- subject knowledge;
- knowledge about techniques/skills;
- involvement with the task.

The teacher also demonstrates an ability to:

- give guidance;
- give direction and focus;
- be both sensitive and aware;
- listen actively;
- protect pupils against disparagement and ridicule;
- recognize when real effort needs further encouragement;
- foster a climate which supports creative ideas.

Creative teaching can be seen as the same as good practice, yet good practice is not necessarily creative teaching. Creative teaching involves a complex interplay between the child, the teacher and the context in such a way that each element is pushing forward, seeking new boundaries, striving towards new territories, always looking to extend in the search for something new. Teachers increasingly recognize the need to adopt more creative strategies towards the management of the curriculum and to consider contexts which provide a more creative framework for teaching and learning. They are keen to encourage children to be more creative and to develop strategies they can use to support and extend children's natural creative energies.

These are the central issues addressed throughout the six chapters of this book, each of which delves into one of the strands mentioned earlier. The chapters have similar structures, each beginning with a series of short cameos of teaching and learning situations which illuminate the underlying principles in relation to children, teachers and the context. Chapters conclude with a summary, together with some practical advice for teachers.

Because assessment and strategies for change are key issues for all primary teachers, they are integral to the concepts discussed in each chapter. My stance on this has been influenced by many factors drawn from several sources, including:

- the principle of profiling children's learning, and involving them and their parents in the process (Ackers 1994);
- the idea of 'continuous assessment as an aid to the learning process' (Ofsted 1993b: 23);
- the notion of starting from where the child currently is in their understanding (Bruce 1988: 23) and of avoiding labelling (Gipps *et al.* 1995: 13);
- the assessment of children's learning which honours their rights and interests (Drummond 1993: 13).

Considering assessment in these ways will enable key questions to be posed. In answering these, a profile of the child's creativity can be built up. Creativity cannot be assessed as an entity or in the same way as subject areas, though monitoring progress and development is essential in such a subjective and personal field of learning. Children can and should be involved to a large extent in monitoring their own creative progress, and practical ways are suggested throughout the book.

No discussion of theory can ever be separated from practical implications; therefore some clear, tried-and-tested strategies are described which will enable the reader to adopt a more creative approach to teaching and learning. Chapters provide accessible suggestions for change in each of the six focus areas. None of them requires a large amount of effort, expensive extra resources or changes in legislation. All of the strategies can be adopted now: they require only a little will and a lot of creative thinking!

Chapter 1 considers creativity as a form of learning and the way in which it can enrich and develop learning in all areas of the curriculum. Because it enables children to communicate and express themselves with or without words, behaving in a creative way can increase children's confidence. The development of literacy and numeracy skills are shown to benefit if teachers adopt a more creative approach to teaching and learning.

Chapter 2 considers the representational aspect of creativity by addressing the notion that creativity is an entitlement for all children. Representation crosses language and cultural barriers yet is still culturally defined. Suggestions for management are given alongside indications of the way in which the social context can be used to enhance equal opportunities.

The strand of productivity is discussed in Chapter 3 by considering the importance of the creative process in helping children to reflect, modify their ideas and develop concentration, together with the role of the creative 'product' (which for many teachers is the main feature of creative activities). Ways of overcoming some of the social, managerial and behavioural constraints are suggested so that teachers can feel more confident in giving time to the creative process. Following this, Chapter 4 is concerned with the way in which imagination acts as a driving force behind creative productivity. This includes the role of play in helping children to understand, to represent the world in a safe way, to view life through other perspectives, and to enable pride and self-esteem to be enhanced. Some of the links between imagination and non-conformity are considered in the light of social constraints and the formality of the school system, picking up the strand of originality which forms the basis of Chapter 5. The nature–nurture debate is considered, as is the teacher's role in promoting creativity, in particular the development of appropriate attitudes and the promotion of a suitable context. The basic argument is that creative thinking and problem solving provide a strategy for dealing with change and can be developed by teacher and child alike.

In the final chapter, we take up the last strand and explore why working with nature is important for children, and how this approach can be extended in the classroom to enhance the development of the whole child, socially, physically and intellectually. Practical ideas for enhancing the school grounds and using the local community are included.

The central tenet of this book is that creativity is essential to every child's development. It is a vital ingredient in successful teaching. Since the inception of a legislated curriculum in this country, creativity has not received the focus it deserves. The time is now ripe for a return to recognizing the central importance of creativity to learning. It is my intention to enable readers to re-affirm their beliefs in holistic learning, to make the wealth of knowledge about creativity more easily accessible and, above all, to generate enthusiasm in readers to provide more opportunities to develop creativity in children – and in themselves.

1

'This creative messing about is all very well, but what about the 3 Rs?'

Creativity and learning

Cameo 1

Nicola, aged 7, is busy in the art corner. She is making a card. She has decided to use a variety of materials to stick to the front – pieces of material cut raggedly, some sequins, scraps of coloured paper, wool, lentils and seeds. She is totally absorbed in her efforts, working alone, not noticing that it is time to clear up. She appears to be attracted to the patterns she is making. She opens the finished card and writes carefully 'to my teacher . . . love from Nicola'. She then fits the card tightly inside an envelope she has made earlier. Several of her finished envelopes are nearby.

Cameo 2

Children in a Year 4 class are studying aspects about Russia. The teacher has decided to introduce the topic in an imaginative way. The children begin by examining a wooden bear puppet which can be manipulated by strings, an artefact made in Russia. The children are encouraged to consider its aesthetic qualities, the way it has been crafted and to consider their feelings about it. Their emotional response to the topic is immediate: 'I like the way the lines have been cut on the bear to make it look like fur'; 'I think the person who made it really cared about making it'. The class sit in a circle on the floor. The bear is passed around the circle with each child commenting on some aspect. The teacher acts as a scribe, noting the comments on a large sheet of paper. By using this approach, the teacher shows that he is sensitive to the children's responses and gives value to each child's feelings. It is this emotional involvement in the topic which will give it permanence in each child's memory.

Cameo 3

Duncan, 20 months old, picks up his mother's fish slice and toddles around the living room waving it at objects in the room, at the same time as muttering 'issy, issy, issy'. He repeats this action for 20–25 minutes, happily absorbed in his own world and oblivious to outside factors. He assumes that the adults in the room are fully conversant with his actions. Indeed they are, since they have recognized that Duncan is casting spells upon the various objects and is enacting the role of a wizard, which he has previously seen on television.

Cameo 4

A group of Year 1 children are sitting on the carpet randomly sorting a box of Lego. The bricks are scattered in various piles. Susie has noticed the lack of Lego people and Matt has bemoaned the lack of Lego wheels. When they report this to their teacher, she immediately sees the potential for some investigative work which will allow them to use a little creativity to solve this problem. Which pieces are missing? What could have happened to them? The children are intrigued and begin to speculate. 'Someone might have taken them home to put in their own Lego set to play with'; 'I think they've hidden the Lego under the cupboard and under the table'; 'Somebody might have put them in their pocket'; 'I thought that some people like Lego and they haven't got Lego at home so they take them.' These creative suggestions later lead to some exciting written work.

Introduction

Creativity is playing a part in the learning of all the children in the cameos. We shall see in this chapter just what an important contribution creativity can make to learning across the curriculum. By appealing to the emotional and aesthetic responses to learning, creativity will enhance understanding and promote development. It harnesses parts of the brain additional to the purely cognitive. By developing and using all the brain's powers learning will be maximized (Brierley 1984). This chapter considers some of the ways in which young children learn, how teachers can move to a more creative approach which will also enhance literacy and numeracy, and means of developing a more creative context. Firstly, let us look at children's learning.

Creativity, learning and the child

None of the children in the cameos is involved in sitting silently at desks performing written tasks. Although desk-bound learning has its place in developing basic skills and good learning habits, over-concentration on this can prevent us from seeing the potential of more active and creative approaches. In order to learn children have first to be 'engaged'; in other words they have to be sufficiently motivated to start and then to persevere with a task (Edwards and Knight 1994). In all the cameos this is the most obvious factor: all the children are absorbed in their activities for a considerable period of time. Consider how Duncan is kept involved through his role play for over 20 minutes. He is at an age when many people believe that 'young children can't concentrate' and that they have 'butterfly minds'. This is a myth which should be instantly challenged. Children who are interested concentrate; if they see the relevance of the activity they will engage in it until they feel they have mastered it. They seem possessed of an inner drive which channels their innate curiosity towards finding the most appropriate way of satisfying it. For example, if they are interested in finding out about rotation then children will explore things that turn: commonly cars, pull-along toys, wheels, cogs, tops, rolling cylinders down slopes and rotating arms and hands windmill-style.

Rotation is one of the more common schemas which govern young children's interest, a schema being a pattern of behaviour involving a systematic exploration of abstract ideas. The somewhat strange actions of young children who, like Duncan, appear to be involved in repetition of 'meaningless' actions can be interpreted as the child's way of making sense of a particular schema or concept. Nicola, too, is working through the concept of enveloping, seemingly fascinated by making a run of cards and letters and putting them in envelopes of all shapes and sizes. Once both children have explored their ideas fully they will move on to other, new ideas, which may involve these same schemas or different ones.

In what sense are the children being creative or learning? The way in which we view learning will affect our views of creativity. Whether or not we perceive that learning is taking place in the cameos and what value we place on that learning depends very much on our knowledge of learning theory. A brief consideration of three very influential learning theorists will be helpful here.

Piaget

Piaget viewed children's thinking as qualitatively different from that of adults (Piaget 1973). Several factors influence intellectual growth: experience, maturation, social transmission and, most fundamentally, equilibrium (finding the balance between things previously understood and those yet to be understood). When considering the notion of artistic, imaginative and aesthetic development, Piaget's stages of development aid our under-standing of the artistic process (Lowenfeld and Brittain 1982: 43). Figure 1.1 outlines the main stages.

Piaget deemed these stages to be hierarchical in that the more advanced stages could not be reached without passing through the earlier ones. Crucially, he saw continuity in this development. A more detailed account can be found in Donaldson (1978: 129–45). While much of Piaget's work can be seen to have limita-tions owing to the context and rationale which Piaget employed (Donaldson 1978) – indeed, he has often been misinterpreted by

---

Sensori-motor (0–2) – the child is concerned here with its own percep-tual functions.

Pre-operational (2–6) – the child learns to represent the world by sym-bols, with no real concepts and no understanding of causal relation-ships.

Concrete operations (7–11) – the child begins to think logically about things she or he has experienced and develops reasoning about size, weight and number.

Formal operations (11–15 onwards) – the child is able to manipulate propositions or ideas.

Figure 1.1 Piaget's stages of development

teachers – his ideas on the accommodation and assimilation of knowledge are very useful when considering how children develop concepts and make sense of the environment. Duncan and Nicola are involved in tasks which involve pattern and repetition which help them gradually to make logical patterns and sequences marrying earlier and current understandings. The children involved with the bear puppet and the Lego draw extensively on their previous knowledge and experience of the world in order to master new concepts.

Piaget's emphasis on action and self-directed problem solving supports a creative approach and creative activities which involve practical and first-hand experiences. Nicola is certainly self-directed and the Lego group are engaged in problem solving which motivates their learning.

Bruner

Bruner is concerned with the way in which children make sense of their world and the way in which meaning is ascribed to language and thought. He sees the acquisition of knowledge and understanding as having three distinct aspects, or forms of representation: the enactive, the iconic and the symbolic (Bruner 1975: 11). Figure 1.2 gives a brief summary.

All learning involves an interaction between the three forms of representation. Depending on the amount of a person's previous experience, they will lean more heavily upon one form or another. For example, when meeting new material for the first time the enactive stage will tend to predominate. If we consider our own learning we can see that learning to drive a car involves a considerable amount of enactive learning when we handle the car and experience driving as a physical experience, before internalizing an image of the driving process – 'iconic' – which later enables us to explain the process orally – 'symbolic'. When considering the nature of creative development, Bruner's process provides us

---

Enactive – based on action

Iconic – the action is replaced by an image

Symbolic – expressed through language

Figure 1.2 Bruner's three forms of representation

with a most useful framework – it underlies many examples throughout this book.

Though there are elements of Bruner's work which complement Piaget's – for example in the acquisition of new knowledge and the reassessment of previous knowledge which parallels Piaget's accommodation and assimilation – there are fundamental differences. Piaget's stages have led to the idea of 'readiness', that is, of a child being 'ready' for the next stage. Bruner's modes of representation operate simultaneously and, therefore, provided the approach is appropriate, any child can learn any concept at any time.

The two theorists differ widely in relation to their views on the role of the social-cultural context. Piaget approached his study of human behaviour as a biological process: man was to be viewed as a member of the animal species and that observed traits would hold true for all members of the species. Bruner, on the other hand, considers that all learning takes place in a cultural context, and that this interplay between the individual and their social setting accounts for the wide variance in knowledge and understanding (Bruner 1990). Bruner describes the different processes that are implicated in creative problem solving (Wood 1988: 8), and lays a greater emphasis on language, communication and instruction. He is interested in the nature of creative thinking and originality and the way that we are able to go beyond the information that we have in order to invent codes and rules. 'Learning involves the search for pattern, regularity and predictability' (Wood 1988: 35). Thus the repetition engaged in by both Duncan and Nicola is vital to the establishment of learning patterns.

Vygotsky

Vygotsky was particularly interested in the transmission of human culture and the way in which images conveyed through, for example, art, literature and history influence this process (Wood 1988: 10). Like Bruner, Vygotsky is concerned with the way in which language influences learning and the way in which learning is enhanced by social interaction. His ideas of the 'zone of proximal development' (Vygotsky 1978) whereby the learner is helped towards a higher level of performance through the support of his peers or his teacher is similar to Bruner's idea of 'scaffolding' learning. Looking at the social context of learning through reference to Bruner and Vygotsky will enable us to see how creativity may flourish if that context is also creative.

The children in Cameo 2 are involved in several aspects of creativity which enhance their learning. Firstly they use their senses to engage in 'enactive' learning, using the skill of close observation to arrive at an understanding about the artefact; about similarity and difference; how the object feels, smells, looks, even tastes; what are its properties and how it might be used. Secondly they express emotional responses to it and exercise aesthetic judgements; thirdly they express their ideas in a variety of forms – drawing, writing, model making and in discussion. The children have time to experience the object through handling it, time to internalize their ideas and then time to express them. They are learning in a social context; one which is secure and supportive because the circle enhances cooperation and self-discipline (see Strategies for Change section). This enables a very personal response to be used to advance learning not only about aesthetic qualities, but also about mathematical concepts and language. The class need to respond personally before they can write freely about it with understanding and relevance. Though this is also an example about good practice, as noted in the Introduction, the reliance upon an emotional response, the use of the expressive arts and the exercise of aesthetic judgements make this good creative teaching.

The children playing with the Lego have again been supported by the social context. Their learning has been 'scaffolded' by the teacher in that she has moved their observations onto a higher plane by setting the investigation and supporting children's findings by showing them how to record in a variety of ways. She has advanced the learning of other children in the class through sharing the findings and ways of recording, and making a class book. The children in the group have supported each other throughout the task, counting, sorting and recording in a collaborative way. The basis of the learning here has developed from a creative problem-solving approach.

The self-directed nature of the learning in which Nicola, Duncan and initially the group in Cameo 4 are involved means that they are motivated to discover new ideas (Edwards and Knight 1994). Nicola is able to explore a variety of materials and to understand something about their nature. She is learning about fixing materials, about the way in which cards open and where the writing should go. She is learning about measurement, spatial awareness, how the card fits into the envelope, about the purpose for cards and of the feelings evoked by giving and receiving. Duncan is able to master the idea of having some control over his environment through adopting the role of the wizard. He is making sense of actions he has seen on television and is trying them out in order to understand them. He is building up an awareness of the relationship between language and action with his 'spells'. The Lego group have initially discovered a problem and are eager to set about solving it: the teacher intervenes sensitively to move their learning on. The children's ideas about learning would seem to be very clear to them.

How can teachers bring about such motivation in setting their learning objectives?

Creativity, learning and the teacher

Seeing the benefits of creativity

Teachers initially might be worried that this could all just be seen as 'messing about'. Nicola, Duncan and the Lego group could be seen as 'just playing'; the language circle could be seen as an excuse to keep the children occupied by handling a toy. They might feel that there is no time for all this, that the children need to be getting on with formalized curriculum learning. Indeed, there are many pressures on teachers to find the simplest and most straightforward way of meeting attainment targets (Campbell *et al.* 1993; Woods 1995). Fortunately many teachers resist, realizing that this means throwing away many practices which form the basis of good teaching. Learning involves more than just being able to say a child has done a particular task and now appears to be at a particular level. It involves complex interactions between the child, the teacher and the context. Activities which appear to be purely about play or about creativity need to be unravelled so that we can see that they involve more than rote learning, copying or other pencil and paper tasks which may promote little challenge.

Creativity can be seen as a form of intelligence. Gardner (1978) regards it as one of the 'multiple intelligences' which cover various functions of the brain. It is a necessary and vital component without which the learner only operates on a narrow cognitive level. The creative aspect of the brain can help to explain and interpret abstract concepts, thus enabling the child to have a greater mastery, particularly in such subjects as mathematics and science which are often difficult to understand. The teacher in Cameo 2 is using a response to creativity in order to help the children understand the complexities of how and why something is made. She helps them to express their ideas and feelings by scaffolding their learning. She knows that the language skills gained here will form an excellent foundation for the writing and reading which follows on. When the children write about the Russian artefacts they will have an understanding of them as a result of this approach. Similarly the teacher has structured the Lego sorting to include numeracy, measurement, comparison, classification and data collection. The task has a purpose, it poses a problem which children need to solve, and it uses everyday, practical materials in an active situation. This enables the children to explore the materials in their own time and pace, making learning meaningful and exciting.

Teachers can adopt approaches to teaching which will encourage problem solving and investigation, drawing upon children's natural curiosity and desire to learn. Problem solving allows children to use their imagination, to try out their ideas and to think about a variety of possibilities. Because problem solving uses these elements of creativity it allows children some degree of self-direction. Anghileri (1995) shows how a creative approach has definite benefits for children's mathematical development.

Similarly they can allow time for reflection, the part of the creative process which helps to generate ideas when the imagination is brought into play. They can ensure that this thinking time is built into their plans. Teachers obviously make the decisions over what is taught and the amount of time to be devoted by each child to particular areas, but they can make learning more accessible to children by allowing them a degree of self-initiated learning. Teachers and children can share learning through discussion of the children's learning diaries (see Strategies for Change section).

Many teachers are keen to adopt a more holistic approach to the curriculum as they have seen how this gives children greater opportunities for reaching learning targets. Individual attainment targets can be met several times in different tasks, in a variety of ways. Teachers have more time to develop their ideas since one theme may cover the entire term's targets across the curriculum. Since teachers always need to justify their actions it helps if we can show that we are meeting the needs of the core curriculum in most of our work. It can be useful to show that the following creative ways of working which promote creativity will also enhance literacy and numeracy.

Close observation

Close observation is a technique much used in art to enhance drawing and painting skills (Robinson 1989). It is a skill which is vital to other areas of the curriculum as it heightens perception and enables children to focus sharply, helping them to study details of objects in greater depth. It aids science skills as it encourages accurate observation and analysis of processes (Harlen 1992); in maths it promotes the observation of patterns. If discussion accompanies close observation (as shown in Cameo 2) then it will greatly aid language and literacy development. In Cameo 4 the children were using close observation skills in order to help them sort accurately and to perceive small details of difference. Regular opportunities for close observational work are needed to develop visual and auditory discrimination. Games such as 'I-spy' and 'What's that sound?' enhance such skills and are well directed time fillers for odd moments. Figure 1.3 shows the degree of concentration generated by close observational work in science and the sharp focus that can be obtained from using practical materials for first-hand experience.

Cross-curricular themes

The four cross-curricular themes (NCC 1990a, b, c, d) noted in Figure 1.4 were designed to be taught alongside the other curriculum areas. They embrace important elements. These themes enable programmes of work to be planned for primary children which relate subject areas in a meaningful way. For example, a study of citizenship encourages:

- sharing ideas about rights and responsibilities;
- problem solving and using the thinking part of the creative process;
- opportunities for writing, particularly first-hand accounts and drama;

Figure 1.3 Close observation encourages children to concentrate

- the collection of statistics on various data;
- the use of design and technology to explore ways in which changes can be made.

The themes are particularly appropriate for use at primary level since they cover not only areas of immediate interest and relevance, but because they approach learning as a holistic body of knowledge rather than compartmentalized subjects (Bruce 1987; David *et al.* 1993; Gammage and Meighan 1993). They provide excellent ways of giving children meaningful literacy and numeracy experiences through problem solving, drama and cre-

---

National Curriculum Council (1990a) *Curriculum Guidance 4: Education for Economic and Industrial Understanding.*

National Curriculum Council (1990b) *Curriculum Guidance 5: Health Education.*

National Curriculum Council (1990c) *Curriculum Guidance 7: Environmental Education.*

National Curriculum Council (1990d) *Curriculum Guidance 8: Citizenship.*

Figure 1.4 National Curriculum cross-curricular themes

ative writing. Cross-curricular themes can often be introduced through an appropriate story.

Working through stories

Indeed stories are useful starting points for all areas of the curriculum (Sylvester 1991; National Council for Educational Technology 1992). They provide a means of discussing issues (Rowe and Newton 1994) and can be used to begin the development of thinking about issues (Lipman 1991). Not only does this increase interest in literacy, but it provides a suitable vehicle for exploration of other expressive arts. Dramatizing a story immediately gives it more meaning and enables the children to take ownership of it. Duncan is adapting the story of the wizard he has seen on television into his own drama. Nicola is involved not only in creating the card, but in the dramatized story of posting it to her teacher. Both children are engaged in a form of role play which develops naturally from stories. Stories provide inspiration for art work which in turn increases familiarity with story structures.

In addition to stories from a variety of literary heritages, stories chosen from those well known through performance, such as Swan Lake or Peer Gynt, add a new dimension to the study of music and dance. Retelling of stories gives children the chance to express their ideas in their own way and increases motivation alongside literacy and oral skills. As children become familiar with the various elements of a particular story they may begin to restructure them; the original characters may be used in new settings; the original plot may be used with new characters (Egan 1988). Children will absorb the underlying structures and make the stories their own.

It can be advantageous to extend this thinking and skills further by linking work from the same author, the same genre or a historical period, so that similarities and differences can be explored in depth. Stories can also be a middle part of a project arising out of other work, as in the case of Lego sorting in Cameo 4. The book made from the children's discoveries stimulated further writing about the children's ideas of what had happened, thus neatly linking reality with imagination.

Working thematically

Literacy will be more meaningful if it is part of a purposeful context (Graves 1983). Creative thinking skills developed through working thematically will greatly aid the mastery of basic reading and writing skills. Creative work can be developed further by encouraging children to explore links and connections and to see less obvious combinations, rather than following one narrow line of thought. In working thematically and using topics the teacher can encourage children to make sense of their experiences by finding these links and enabling them to see the component parts of the whole (Blenkin and Kelly 1994).

For example in looking at Russian artefacts the children studied one item at a time, using close observation and language skills in order to get to the heart of what made up the 'Russian-ness' of each artefact. At the end of several weeks the children were able to categorize the particular Russian style of the artefacts and could pick out the salient characteristics. This aspect of concept formation is often overlooked. Children and adults may be very familiar with some concepts such as Lego but be quite unable to itemize what makes Lego distinct from other forms of building bricks. We may be familiar with citrus fruits, but saying what makes citrus fruits distinct from other fruits may be less easy. All broad classifications can only be understood by a thorough knowledge of the component parts (Willig 1990). The teacher's task is to break down the complexity of the whole into easily manageable areas for learning. This is the process Bruner refers to when he talks of all subjects as being within the grasp of anyone so long as the process is made at the right level.

We can provide opportunities for working in this way in order to develop a particular set of skills and understanding. Figure 1.5 shows how a discussion about individual citrus fruits has led to some important conceptual discoveries which span several subject areas. There is a sense of excitement to be generated by anchoring yourself firmly to a theme and then sparking off learning in many directions. We can also make some of the more mundane tasks (such as spelling, number bonds and handwriting practice) more fun, and we can increase motivation if we put them into a context with a purpose and relate them to the current theme.

Working with themes does not deny that 'subjects are a necessary feature of the primary curriculum' (Alexander *et al.* 1992: 1); indeed, the concepts embedded within subjects are seen as essential. With younger children this subject depth can be instigated if themes themselves are developed from a depth of sub-

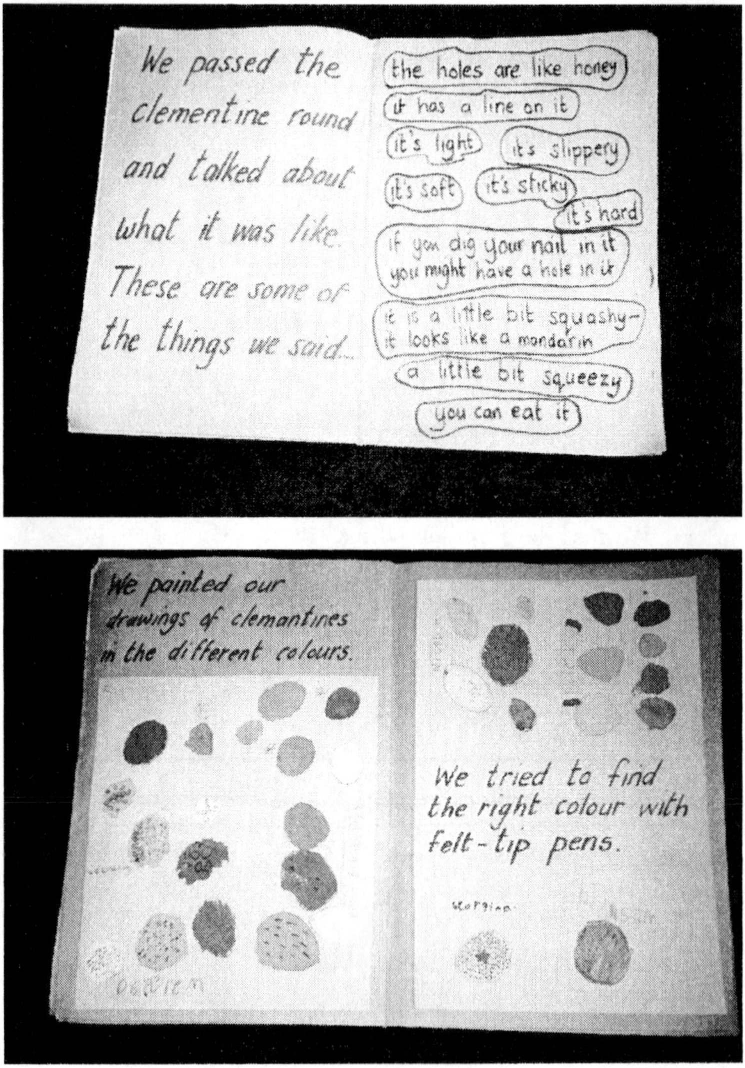

We passed the clementine round and talked about what it was like. These are some of the things we said...

the holes are like honey
it has a line on it
it's light
it's slippery
it's soft
it's sticky
it's hard
if you dig your nail in it you might have a hole in it
it is a little bit squashy—
it looks like a mandarin
a little bit squeezy
you can eat it

We painted our drawings of clementines in the different colours.

We tried to find the right colour with felt-tip pens.

Figure 1.5 Working thematically enables children to acquire a broad understanding of concepts

ject knowledge. Subject divisions are not necessarily inconsistent with a child's view of the world (p. 17), but since babies are not born with them, they must be taught to see subjects as socially organized concepts affected by cultural perceptions. As subject divisions are not finite, making links across them can be creatively productive. Inventions have resulted from this sort of conceptual leap. Most great creative thinkers, such as Leonardo da Vinci, have been people whose ideas and inventions overlapped subject boundaries.

Subject divisions should not be confused with subject knowledge; the former are arbitrary, the latter essential. Depth of subject knowledge provides 'appropriate learning objectives' indicated as crucial to topic learning by the Office for Standards in Education (1993c: 18).

Understanding concept development

We can all sometimes find it difficult to plan thematic work thoroughly. We may be unsure of exactly what is meant by the terms 'concepts', 'attitudes', 'skills' and 'knowledge' (CASK) the elements of learning referred to by HMI (DES 1985a). Figure 1.6 gives useful definitions.

'Concept' is the element which seems to present the most problems as it is often assumed that concepts are somehow static. The idea that concept acquisition is an ongoing process which begins at birth and continues throughout life (Willig 1990) seems to be a hard one to grasp. It is easy to think that, as a result of being taught a concept, for example the number ten, it is then learnt

---

Concepts – generalisations which help to classify and organise knowledge and experiences and to predict.

Attitudes – expressions of values and personal qualities which determine behaviour in a variety of situations.

Skills – the capacity or competence to perform a task or activity.

Knowledge – the information required in order to carry out a task or to understand a concept.

Figure 1.6   The learning elements
Source: DES (1985a).

once and for all. In fact not only does it take a child a long time to grasp the concept of ten-ness, but because the concept is so context-dependent (Hughes 1981), ideas about ten will continue to extend and develop throughout life as the child gains new knowledge and experience. In Cameo 2 the teacher's concept of the Russian bear artefact will differ from the children's because of his greater knowledge and understanding of the USSR.

If one realizes that concepts continually change and adapt as a result of experience, thoughts and feelings, the importance of developing and expressing creativity can be seen. By learning to feel in new ways and express these ideas we are helping children to deepen their understanding of the world: 'the enrichment of vital personal experience is what education is about' (Yardley 1970: 11). This creative enrichment will enable children to master the basic skills all the more easily.

Creative enrichment needs a particular context in which to flourish, so let us consider that next.

The context for creativity and learning

Creativity, learning and the curriculum

In seeking to be creative teachers may often have to deal with what may seem to be rather unsupportive situations, and a number of social constraints (Fryer 1996: 109). Creative tasks are often perceived to be of lesser importance than reading, writing and number work. The '3 Rs' dominate classroom time in primary schools and have done so for several decades. Yet, despite this, there is a call for more work on the basics, as if mere quantity of time will solve national or local shortcomings in literacy and numeracy. Many teachers argue that approaches to the latter have been too narrow and have failed actively to engage children in learning, and that what is needed is a qualitative approach based on an understanding of the way in which creativity can support and enhance literacy and numeracy.

Creativity and the arts are closely linked through the strand of representation (Figure 1.7). Most people's ideas about creativity immediately conjure up pictures of drawing, painting and playing music. The vast majority of writing about creativity comes under the heading of 'art'. Teachers have sought to raise the status of creativity in schools, arguing that its link to the 'expressive

Figure 1.7   Painting is one of the activities most associated with creativity

arts' means that more rather than less skills are involved. Many teachers would support the ideas of Lowenfeld and Brittain (1982) in considering creativity as part of intellectual activity, hence of high status. Creative people use practical skills to great effect, but also engage in a considerable amount of mental activity through the conceptualization, imagination and expression of their ideas. The highly influential writer on the arts, Herbert Read, gave art very high status, seeing art as the main purpose of education and maintaining that the creative drive was of fundamental importance in shaping our culture (Read 1943). It can therefore be argued that because the 'arts' harness both the practical and the intellectual they are operating on a higher plane than other areas of knowledge, such as the sciences.

Although one might expect that the 'arts' would occupy a more central place in the primary curriculum, they do form a considerable block of time when the subjects of art, music and PE are linked together. Creativity is also vital in other subjects such as science and technology. There is therefore considerable scope for using a creative approach, especially as many teachers have chosen to work holistically. As non-tested subjects the arts may have lower status, but they are free from the pressures to conform which testing inevitably brings. Creativity continues to flourish, because teachers are aware of the way in which it enriches children's lives (in a way which worksheets and workbooks cannot). These teachers share the view that 'at a time when the economic and social climate outside the classroom is far from secure, it becomes even more important for the school to be a place where creativity is allowed to flower' (Pluckrose 1993: 67). The social climate too, seems to be becoming more supportive, with leading firms and industries now calling for a resurgence of creative thinking in order to 'harness new ideas to retain a competitive advantage' (de Bono 1996) in a similar way to the USA in the 1960s (Torrance 1962, 1963).

In 1996 the Schools Curriculum and Assessment Authority (SCAA) published a new curriculum for the under-fives which took into account the way in which children's learning takes place across a broad band of subject areas. It is based on the 1985 DES model of the curriculum (Figure 1.8) which gives eight areas of experience, but these have been further refined to give six areas

---

The eight areas of experience

Linguistic and literary

Mathematical

Scientific

Technological

Human and social

Aesthetic and creative

Moral

Spiritual

Figure 1.8 DES (1985) model of the curriculum
Source: DES (1985a).

of development, entitled Desirable Outcomes for Children's Learning (DOCLs). It closely parallels Gardner's multiple intelligences (1993) and thus relates areas of learning to cognitive functioning.

DOCLs give equal status to each of the areas of development, giving creativity development an important place. Inspections ensure that this area is covered by all providers on a daily basis. The document reflects much earlier government reports which gave greater weight to creative development, such as the Hadow Report (Board of Education 1938). Although this report's concern and understanding of young children's development has not subsequently been superseded, its mention of the importance of 'the expression of children's interest in pattern and feeling for rhythm' (p. 128) is reflected in the DOCLs' creative development section in the words 'Children explore sound, colour, texture, shape form and space in two and three dimensions . . . Through art, music, dance, stories and imaginative play, they show an increasing ability to use their imagination, to listen and to observe' (SCAA 1996: 4). Similarly some of the concerns for the developmental needs of young children – including their creative development expressed in the Plowden Report (DES 1967) and the Rumbold Report (DES 1990) which described high quality practice in the pre-school years – have been included. The view of the Rumbold Report that 'young children's development should be viewed as a whole and the curriculum should reflect an understanding of this' (para 14: 7) can be seen to be expressed in the under-fives document.

Teachers have shown their creativity by continuing to think of

---

The six areas of development

Personal and social development

Language and literacy

Mathematics

Knowledge and understanding of the world

Physical development

Creative development

Figure 1.9 The six areas of learning (DOCLs)
Source: DfEE (1996).

appropriate developmental models to support the legislated curriculum. Further innovative early years curricula can be seen in the schema model adopted by Pen Green Nursery (Bartholomew and Bruce 1993: 3) which uses the areas of music, English, maths, geography, science and technology, drama, history, dance, art and movement in 'lines of direction' intended to promote the overall schema of rotation (p. 48). As indicated earlier, children think in terms of concepts or 'schemas' which go beyond subject boundaries and reflect their thinking about, for example, the schemas of 'trajectory', 'enclosure', 'separation and connection' (Athey 1990: 86; Meade and Cubey 1995). Schema models and theories recognize the way in which subject areas interlock: for example in art and maths, even the vocabulary of line, form and shape, as Gura (1992: 42) points out, are the same for both. The continuing debate about the way in which young children learn enables teachers to explore different approaches and to adapt statutory requirements. There is such a vast body of writing and research within this field to support them that they can feel secure when introducing a greater emphasis on creativity as central to learning in all areas.

Key considerations for assessment

The following checklist is intended to help you to ensure that creativity is being used to enhance learning.

The child

- What elements of mathematical development are demonstrated through creative work and problem solving, for example understanding of shape and space in art work, and understanding of measurement in construction play?
- To what extent does the child use mathematical knowledge in expressing creative ideas and in creative activity, such as counting squares in pattern work?
- How does the child express his/her imagination? through writing? interpreting stories? problem solving?
- Does the child communicate his/her ideas in a variety of ways?
- Is the child confident in expressing these ideas orally as well as through different media?

The teacher

- Are plenty of opportunities provided for thematic work in order to develop creativity?
- Is work developed from the children's needs and interests?
- Are stories used as starting points for creative projects?
- When working in the creative areas of the curriculum, for example dance, drama and painting, are opportunities for mathematical and literacy development being fully explored?

The context

- Are there well resourced language and mathematics areas in the classroom which support creative work?
- Are examples of creative writing and problem solving well displayed?
- Does the classroom allow for large scale construction play, designing and making?
- Is there a well developed role play area to encourage imaginative interpretations of experience?

Strategies for change

The children in Cameo 2 worked in a circle in order to examine and discuss the Russian artefacts. The particular benefits of a circle approach are outlined next.

Eight good reasons for working in circles

1 Each child has equal status and is thus equally valued.
2 Circles enhance self-esteem and social development.
3 The circle is a control mechanism and therefore frees the teacher from a management role.
4 Creative thinking is boosted as each child is required to reflect and to express their ideas.
5 If the teacher acts as scribe, noting down comments she dignifies each child's ideas by making them available to the group.
6 This further boosts self-esteem and aids literacy, as children see language, writing and reading all given meaning.
7 Discussion of feelings around difficult issues can be pursued

(McNamara in Moyles 1995: 167) and to raise awareness (Mosley 1993, 1996).

8 The structure can be used to plan and review work along High/Scope UK lines.

Using learning diaries

Learning diaries enable children to be part of the active learning process. Children should use them to record:

- the work they are undertaking, such as the week's plans;
- what they have achieved during the week – this may be about learning, behaviour or both;
- how they feel about activities, such as events and changes in the weather;
- any worries, problems or things that they feel they need help with.

Guidance for using learning diaries

1 They should form the basis of a regular discussion programme with the teacher and may be used for conferencing.
2 They need to maintain an element of personal privacy as comments may be made which are not for sharing.
3 If children do not wish to share the diaries they should be encouraged to share their thoughts.
4 The diaries should encourage children to identify elements of learning in both the cognitive and affective domains.

Summary

This chapter has explored some ways in which children learn. Children see learning as an active process which involves them in making decisions and having time and space to explore ideas in their own way. The cameos indicated that learning creatively enhances all learning and that what is required is the full engagement of the learner in that process, whether it be in art, maths or writing. Teachers' concerns that they might be seen by others to be wasting valuable time by doing creative work which should be spent on literacy and numeracy have been discussed. Ways of working more holistically in the classroom have been shown to meet the needs of the 3 Rs in more interesting and meaningful ways. In looking at the context we have seen how teachers remain creative in their approach in spite of curriculum changes. Current statutory requirements do not prescribe approaches to teaching and we can therefore reclaim more creativity for our timetables. By so doing we are enhancing children's likelihood of success in the 3 Rs.

In the next chapter we shall look at the way the representation strand of creativity can be met by considering the needs of all children.

2

'They can't all be creative can they?'

Creativity and equal opportunities

Cameo 1

Wayne, aged 6, selects a cotton reel from the box of objects in order to tie it into his piece of cloth. Fiona, his teacher, helps him to tie the string around it. Wayne has cerebral palsy and needs a little help. He watches excitedly as he puts his tied bundle into the bowl of red dye. The other children in the group look equally fascinated. They begin to guess what will happen and are caught up in the experience. At a nearby table Anthony watches intently as the colours of marbling inks diffuse and spread across the tray of water. The expression on his face shows a sense of wonder and concentration. Anthony needs an aid to help him hear. His deafness has enabled him to perceive more sharply, and the visual impact of the science work has a special meaning for him.

Cameo 2

Year 2 children have been to the Imperial War Museum at the weekend to see the exhibition on the commemoration of D-Day. On Monday morning they are keen to discuss this and to draw pictures of the war in their diaries. Margaret, their teacher, allows these ideas to be explored. Over several sessions discussions are held about D-Day and about the Second World War, allowing the class to reflect on whether or not they would have liked to have been in a war. Children's comments range from 'I would not like to leave my family', 'I wouldn't want to be killed' to those who see war as a chance for 'driving a tank' and 'fighting the enemy'. The writing and follow-up work show that boys and girls are equally involved. It was not just a 'boy's subject' in spite of the initial interest from the boys. Indeed, differences of opinion could be seen within gender groups, particularly the boys, who were not all responding in the same way. Scott and Darren expressed a strong and profound disagreement with war and felt quite comfortable in stating this, even though their close friends Ryan, John and Robert thought otherwise. Ryan and his friends explored the idea of war for several days through small, detailed drawings and in so doing came to engage in a more realistic, less fantasized view.

Cameo 3

A Year 4 class are working on the theme music to *EastEnders* which is the piece they have chosen for the annual end of year concert. A group in a corner of the room have listened to a tape and have worked out the roles of the various instruments. They are now practising the various elements of the theme with different instruments. Two children from the local secondary school are working with them to give them some extra technical support. Another group are busy working on the scenery which will form the backdrop to a series of dramatic and musical scenes about *EastEnders*. They are using the large collection of magazine pictures about the programme which forms the main display across one classroom wall. They have access to various video recordings for further reference. Two other groups are working on scripts for the scenes and on the dances which will link them. All the children are eagerly involved and there is the low buzz of busy workers. An unexpected bonus has been an improvement in their formally assessed work.

Cameo 4

The first thing that greets you as you enter Ellen's Year 1 class is the enormous Chinese dragon model along the length of one wall. The children have been learning about Chinese New Year. The room is transformed. Poster displays of Chinese music and dancing are surrounded by examples of children's drawings and paintings of them, and there is a table of musical instruments made by the children. The home corner has been changed into a Chinese take-away with lots of examples of Chinese food and menus in Chinese scripts. The ceiling is hung with kites of all sizes, colours and descriptions. Examples of styles of Chinese costumes are set next to children's pastel drawings of them. Some children are studying a large map of China, while another group is practising Chinese calligraphy with ink and brushes. Another group are examining a model of a Chinese junk and trying to see how it is made.

Introduction

Representation forms a broad strand in creativity and enables all children to have a means of expressing their thoughts and feelings. Meeting the needs of all children, though highly rewarding, places special demands on teachers. As the cameos show, the curriculum is enriched by using the diversity of experience which children bring to school. The arts provide us with an exciting area with which to interpret this experience. This chapter will consider some of the children's individual needs with regard to race, gender, class and special needs in relation to creativity, together with some of the ways in which we, as teachers, can try to meet them.

Creativity is for all

In Cameo 1 we can see how inclusion can ensure that children with special needs benefit from creative work. Cameo 2 indicates that boys and girls may have different needs and interests and need different forms of representation in order to express them. Children's ideas can be challenged and developed by reflection and by considering the feelings of others. Representation can help them do this as the children's drawings about war show. The third cameo shows how children's everyday experiences can be used to spark off creativity: no special talents are needed nor particular notions of culture are suggested. Cameo 4 gives us a small indication of the wealth of aesthetic understanding which can be generated by artwork around festivals and celebrations, which weaves across all curriculum areas.

In considering creativity it is important to establish that all children have equal rights to be creative and to have full access to opportunities within the creative areas of the curriculum. However, all children will not respond to creativity in the same way. The way in which people respond places a value and status on certain qualities and not on others, according to personal and cultural viewpoints. Thus we may not always perceive all children to have equal gifts in relation to creativity and may ascribe these differences to perceived notions of ability, class, race, gender and able-bodiedness. It is all too easy to think of a child who shows a particular gift for ballet as being superior both creatively and intellectually to one who loves to dance but who chooses to dance jazz.

These varied cultural and social perspectives on creativity, which are the result of our own individual experiences and preferences, may be compounded by being differentially delivered to various groups within the classroom (for example, streaming by perceived 'creative ability'), thus perpetuating stereotypes and entrenched views which can lead to underachievement rather than opening up learning. We can easily fall into this trap. The links between the school's role and underachievement have been well documented, 'Schools play an active part in creating children who are more or less educable, more or less knowledgeable, more or less manageable' (Bilton *et al.* 1981: 418). We do this through the process of categorizing children into different groups or types. The issues of race, gender, class, ability and able-bodiedness may underlie our definitions of 'a gifted artist' or those who are 'no good at music'. If we try to unravel individual responses from group responses, as the teacher in Cameo 2 did, then this will help us in our desire not to make pre-judgements.

Creativity, equal opportunities and the child

The child with special needs

The creative arts have a particular place in the education of children with special needs. Children who may not be able to gain access to the curriculum in 'conventional' ways can often achieve this through art and other creative experiences. Both Wayne and Anthony in the first cameo were able to understand scientific principles by exploring the science of colour through creative processes. The first-hand experiences of dyeing and marbling were both manageable and enjoyable activities which allowed them greater access to the core curriculum than might otherwise have been possible.

Using art as a creative vehicle to explain complex concepts can help to avoid the use of art mainly as therapy for special needs children. Piotrowski points out that this can undervalue both art and children with special educational needs. 'There is a curious belief that art is a non-academic subject and therefore must be suitable for so-called non-academic pupils' (1996: 2). In her treatise, she provides a more detailed look at the place of each of the arts areas in relation to special needs children in the ordinary school.

It cannot be denied, however, that children such as Anthony, with a hearing impairment, compensate by greater sensitivity in other senses, thus gaining heightened enjoyment and understanding in visual and tactile experiences. For Anthony the joy resulting from the marbling activity reached a spiritual quality; it was not necessarily greater than an experience he might have had through sound, but it put less strain and stress on him, because he did not have to rely on hearing aids.

Like Wayne, one of the obvious benefits for Anthony of the creative/art activities was that they provided the opportunity for sharing the same experiences as the rest of the children, on the same terms.

Gender differences

There is considerable debate among teachers and others about whether girls and boys perceive things differently and whether they choose to express their ideas in different ways – for example, do girls prefer to draw in a small, detailed way, and do boys favour large scale model making? If they do then how far are such preferences the results of social expectations? The answers are obviously not easy to tease out, but what is clear is that there are far fewer examples of female artists, composers, sculptors and writers than male.

Children will obviously be influenced by role models presented to them. When considering the artistic influences on culture today male domination is still prevalent. Resources available to schools reflect this imbalance. In terms of status, the work of male artists is often seen to be more prestigious than that of females. Great thinkers and inventors presented to children are largely male. Few female artists have made a career from their interests; consequently there has been a lack of social acceptance of their work, which has been seen as a hobby. Victorian ladies, for example, were deemed to be proficient at painting, singing, playing the piano and dancing, yet the fact that many were extremely talented went largely unacknowledged.

This is peculiarly at odds with children's widespread perception of the arts as 'female' when they consider subjects for extended study. Such perceptions may lead to the underperformance of girls in 'male' subjects such as maths and science (French 1990: 71), and to the underperformance of boys in the area of literacy, traditionally seen as an 'arts/female' subject (Hanna 1996). Underachievement can be combated by positive approaches such as the GIST (Girls into Science and Technology) project (Whyte 1986) designed to promote girls' interest in science, and those undertaken to encourage girls to use construction materials and technology (Egan 1990; Sherwin 1990; Ross and Browne 1993). Similarly, girls' apparent lack of interest in maths highlighted through awareness of underperformance (Walden and Walkerdine 1982; Straker 1985; Burton 1986; DES 1989) has resulted in teachers taking positive steps to give girls opportunities in maths, often in single-sex groups (Figure 2.1).

Hanna (1996) suggests that similar projects need to be set up with boys in order to encourage thinking and reflecting skills and language-based, rather than action-based, tasks. The response of

Figure 2.1 Girls enjoy the challenges of science and design and technology as much as boys

Scott and Darren to the war discussion in Cameo 2 would seem to bear this out. Where time is created for discussion and reflection then boys are enabled to move away from their first responses – which often centre on action and supporting their peers – to being more considered and thoughtful.

If children are given opportunities to pursue a variety of activities and creative approaches to learning, and are encouraged at all times to think through ideas, to discuss possibilities, to take risks, and to try out new methods, then many of these gender imbalances may not arise. Children given equal opportunities and experiences will respond on an individual rather than gender basis, as the children showed in their work on the D-Day and war project in the second cameo. We need to ensure that boys are given opportunities to do a lot of fine-detail work and that girls are encouraged to undertake large scale art and craft projects which involve an awareness of large area and space. Representation provides opportunities for the development of both fine and gross motor skills; both should be equally fostered in both gender groups.

Cultural relevance

The Year 4 class in Cameo 3, engaged in a busy learning programme around the musical theme of *EastEnders*, appeared motivated and confident, both essential attitudes needed for learning. A desire to learn and belief in one's ability to learn can be achieved through children understanding the purpose and relevance of the tasks in hand and in being able to see how their own previous experiences engage with the new learning on offer. As teachers, we are very aware that marked differences in response to learning and hence to achievement occur as a result of social class and cultural perceptions, particularly in urban areas (Bash *et al.* 1985). This Year 4 class is in a busy inner city area with a rich cultural and ethnic mix. It is an area largely considered as working class. The creative, musical experiences of children in the area are probably of pop music rather than the classics; and their visual interests are more likely to be sparked by the graphic design and patterns they see all around them rather than the pastoral images of old masters in art galleries.

At first the school ignored this clash between very different views of creativity and the status afforded to 'high culture'. They thought that by presenting the children with classical music and 'art' that they were enriching the children's experience. What they had not realized was that, because much of this was irrelevant to many of the children, they were providing creative experiences for only a few. Creativity had become the province of an elite group for whom this culture had some relevance or particular interest. The other children needed to express their own experiences in ways with which they were familiar in order for them to develop skills of criticism and aesthetic appreciation. By translating the excitement of urban living into the classroom, these Year 4 children could immediately see relevance and relate their experiences to new ones. We can give children a wide diversity of both rural and urban cultural images and help them to note the particular qualities of each. It is vital to remember that urban living, with its emphasis on humans rather than the flora and fauna of nature, is equally a source of inspiration to be explored.

Using a common community experience, that of watching television in order to learn new skills in music and other aspects of performance, the children in Cameo 3 are able to see the links between composing and performing in terms of both music and writing. There is a sense of unity within the class, with each child's particular skills and experiences being valued. Children, teachers and parents work cooperatively. Parents share their children's experiences and are willing and able to support them. The whole community has felt involved, with local groups (such as the Baptist choir and nearby secondary school) offering their help. This sense of home-school unity has engendered high levels of motivation. There are few instances of antisocial and disruptive behaviour. Achievement in the core areas of the curriculum has improved alongside this developing creativity. Through meeting the needs of the children within a creative project, the class has found a way of answering the concerns of the Ofsted inspectors that planning should address the needs of children from disadvantaged backgrounds and focus on raising achievement (Ofsted 1993c: 6).

Artistic expression in schools has been greatly enriched by the inclusion in the curriculum of work relating to other cultures, drawing on the wealth of children's experience. Some of the most exciting work in schools relates to topics on festivals and celebrations which allow for a wide range of representation of cultural ideas and feelings; as Cameo 4 shows, music, dancing, singing, poetry, painting, sculpture and drama are all utilized expressively. Children now have great possibilities for extending their understanding about the way people feel by considering, for example, a range of ideas around 'my special place', because there is a diversity of experience to tap into. Cultural diversity has led to many techniques in representation becoming easily accessible, such as batik, henna drawings, shadow puppets, mime, forms of dance, different musical scales and calligraphy. These techniques, once mastered, can be used creatively, that is, in new ways, enriching and extending ideas and 'pushing forward the boundaries' (Fryer 1996: 123). Out of this creative fusion new forms of music, such as Bhangra, combining traditional Indian music with Western rock music, have arisen. New styles of painting, such as those now in art galleries drawing on the technique of graffiti, show how creativity can act as a catalyst in promoting cultural change. As teachers we can seize these opportunities to ensure that classroom work is inspired by such enrichment and creates new ideas and ways of teaching and learning.

Creativity, equal opportunities and the teacher

Opening up expressive opportunities

As teachers we have a role in offering a variety of means of expression to children and in encouraging all forms of creative representation. Many primary age children find non-verbal expression easier than verbal means, despite the classroom emphasis often given to written language. If children are able to express themselves in a variety of ways, they will have correspondingly extended learning opportunities. The children in Cameo 3 have the opportunity to discover their skills in performing music, singing, composing, choreographing and dancing. They may find that instead of being labelled 'tone deaf' or 'having two left feet', they are able composers who enjoy musical involvement. It would seem sensible for us to build up skills and self-esteem in areas in which the child readily responds, we should capitalize on strengths and interests. The resulting self-esteem will give children greater motivation and willingness to try those areas of the curriculum in which they feel less secure. Many cases of learning difficulty occur in the field of literacy (Lewis 1991) and these difficulties often give rise to emotional and behavioural problems. We all know children for whom an emphasis on reading too early is detrimental, particularly those with special needs who, unable to cope, may become disaffected.

Creative approaches and literacy

In order to increase overall literacy levels, there is a strong argument for teachers spending more time in the classroom on a wider range of activities and approaches as identified in Chapter 1. Skills acquired in other curriculum areas can readily be transferred to literacy. Cortazzi points out that around a third of the time in primary classrooms is spent on writing (1995: 178) yet we know that this is an area which challenges many children. Working in the arts can provide an alternative route to literacy for those who do not write readily. A broad-based approach to the curriculum is needed (Lewis 1991), giving children ample time for discussion, drama, a range of art activities and music and movement. Such activities provide a means for meeting children's social, emotional, intellectual, physical and creative developmental needs, resulting in increased confidence and more motivated approaches to other learning.

As teachers we may, quite naturally, have worries about the management aspects of giving each child creative opportunities. Images of immediate chaos as every child struggles to use scarce resources and the room exploding into a cacophony of sound as children practise instruments concern many of us, as Fryer discovered in her study (1996: 112). Yet despite these worries we will persevere if we are convinced of the importance of creative development. Adopting certain strategies, such as encouraging children to be independent and gaining extra support when possible in order to minimize demands on time, means we can release time and energy to support creative activities.

Encouraging independence

Children need to be very clear about the teacher's learning intentions. If we look more closely at the way in which the class in Cameo 3 is working, we can see that the learning objectives have been shared carefully with the class, the children being given some choice over which activities they pursue and when. The groups are therefore largely self-chosen. As tasks are taking place, smaller groups report back to the larger one. It is clear what skills and knowledge are being utilized. Children who have not yet completed tasks have found out from their peers what is involved. If children change over groups in order to undertake a different task, it is the children who explain the task to each other. This independence enables the teacher to deal with explaining new learning and developing new ideas as they arise, a pattern of working only possible if the teacher has given thought to the way in which children need to be trained into working creatively and independently.

Extending peer group support

Older children can assist younger children with their learning and provide the scaffolding of knowledge which both Bruner and Vygotsky see as one of the main ways of extending learning (see Chapter 1). This is a two-way process, since in helping a younger one the older child has to explain and demonstrate knowledge and skill, thus consolidating their own understanding. Peer group support can free the teacher from many routine tasks. Children who have mastered a skill or technique, as with the marbling in Cameo 1, are able to pass on that experience and skill to others. A bonus is that the teacher can free time to assess learning outcomes for both sets of peers.

Working with parents

Help provided by parents and other community members is always welcome. If volunteers are willing to work on a regular basis, then it is possible to reorganize working groups to accommodate more creative work. The support of parents and local adults enabled the class in Cameo 3 to extend the curriculum on offer. The teacher's task is made easier if both home and school share the same values and aims for their children. It therefore follows that when such harmony is achieved there are more opportunities for active and creative learning experiences. Teachers will be encouraged to tackle activities, such as drama and working with instruments, if they are secure in the knowledge that behavioural problems are likely to be rare. When teachers share their learning objectives with parents they usually find many parents willing to work alongside groups in the classroom on creative tasks such as modelling or cooking, and many who will support projects, bringing in artefacts, talking about their experiences or helping with tasks like costume design for productions. Listening to parents about their ideas has not only helped to break down potential stereotypes about home and school, but has given both teachers and parents an understanding of the complexities of their roles (Bastiani and Wolfendale 1996). Where teachers are clearly from a different social class or ethnic background to the children and parents this can be of particular benefit and result in the sharing of knowledge and ideas, for example about community events, such as a carnival, which can stimulate classroom work in the expressive arts.

Monitoring and assessing balance

When children work more independently, teachers can direct more of their time towards monitoring classroom behaviour and response. In Cameo 2, we saw how Margaret's ability to observe her children closely, to listen to them and to allow the children time to discuss and extend their ideas, led to more reflective children with less gender-stereotypical behaviour. If we are to provide for the creative needs of all children we must make time to listen, observe and monitor creative thinking, attitudes and progress on a regular basis.

Both long and short term planning needs to take into account the variety of activities to be offered and the approach to be used. This may mean making provision for single-sex groups to work in particular areas, such as giving all-girl groups enhanced opportunities to develop problem-solving skills without the boys. Similarly, children with particular needs or gifts may need to be given tasks together from time to time. Children's cultural experiences can be drawn upon and extended; planning in advance helps to make sure these aspects are covered. Also thematic work (see Chapter 1) needs to be planned to ensure that both curricular and individual needs are met. Both long and short term plans can be used to indicate how the issues of gender, race, culture and SEN are going to be addressed. This can provide a reminder of just what a web of diverse experience there is within the class which teachers can utilize for a wide range of creative and representational activities.

Examining our own attitudes

It is also useful from time to time to consider the way in which we may be conveying attitudes and expectations about creativity through the 'hidden curriculum'. For example, cultural bias towards creativity can be expressed in such comments as 'I don't know how you can bear to listen to that!' or 'What awful colour combinations – trees aren't that colour'. Maybe in some parts of the world trees *are* that colour. It is easy for us to forget that perhaps many people like the colour combinations or the music we have so hastily dismissed. However, our disapproval has been inadvertently transmitted to the child. Children may also come across such attitudes outside school, within society and from the media. They may even be aware of some stereotypical views, for example that opera is only for rich people.

Stereotyping

The Oxford Dictionary (1979) defines the word 'stereotype' in two ways: as a printing plate cast from a mould of type, or as an idea of character that is standardized in a conventional form without individuality. What is quite clear is that *stereotyping is the very antithesis of a creative approach* for all. The definition 'the printing plate cast', when applied to the notion of people, gives us a 'standardized' type 'without individuality'. This is totally opposite to the view that creativity is based on 'the fulfilment of individual potential which has always been at the heart of a good education system' (Measor and Sikes 1992: 145). In order to open up creative potential in the classroom we need to be very aware of the way in which stereotyping has affected these different groups in the past. Entitlement for all children is now enshrined in law (for example, Sex Discrimination Act 1975; Race Relations Act 1976; Education Reform Act 1988; Disability Discrimination Act 1995). As teachers we must adopt classroom strategies to combat the particular prejudices that are transmitted about creativity which may prevent some children from fulfilling their entitlement.

Many stereotypes about racial characteristics affect the way children both perceive creativity and the way in which they subsequently perform. For example, many black children of Afro-Caribbean descent are seen as either very musical, particularly with regard to drums, or very active physically and 'good at sports', rather than showing ability in more academic subjects. It is often hard for teachers to combat the effect of some of these deeply held social stereotypes (even though they are positive ones) but choosing themes which celebrate cultural diversity is one way of achieving this. Teachers are very aware of the need to have high expectations of ethnic minority pupils since the effects of low teacher expectations have been amply demonstrated by studies such as Milner (1983) and the Swann Report (HMSO 1985b). They are also well aware of the way in which children tend to live up to expectations in a 'self-fulfilling prophecy' (Rist 1970). High expectations can have the crucial effect of increasing a child's creative chances. Children who are not categorized as being a particular type, or as having particular characteristics will generally have more creative freedom and wider experiences.

It is worth reminding ourselves that social expectations which children tend to share about particular ethnic groups, for example that Asian and Chinese groups are hard-working, clever and likely to succeed (Brain and Martin 1983), can affect these children's self-esteem if they do not happen to fit the stereotype. Similarly, broad categorizations about ethnic groups, for example making assumptions that Greek Cypriots are more likely to be 'Western' in outlook than Turkish Cypriots (Beetlestone 1985), may lead children to feel confused about their own identity. This will make it harder for them to express their beliefs and feelings, and thus influence their creativity. Black role models can be found in the field of the arts, particularly the pop culture of music, dance, film and modelling, thus providing continuing social evidence that these perceptions have validity. There are a wealth of reasons why we need to continue to develop all aspects of creativity within all children, so that they can respond to life as individuals and find a means of expressing their ideas in a purposeful and meaningful way whatever their culture, gender, ethnicity, faith or other background.

In the next section we look at the way we can extend children's views about creativity through the media.

The context for creativity and equal opportunities

Children are exposed to large amounts of popular culture which need to be explored in the classroom, both as a source of creative

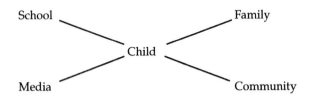

Figure 2.2   Agents of socialization

imagery, and in enabling children to understand how notions of status arise. In trying to promote a learning programme for every child it can be useful to explore with children some of the ways in which attitudes are formed and affect creativity, so that the children are enabled to exercise both understanding and judgement. A diagrammatic explanation is given in Figure 2.2.

As an example, in spite of the inclusion of folk and popular music in the National Curriculum alongside that from the European 'classical' tradition, the issue of cultural superiority with regard to music remains. These judgements affect the relevance, enjoyment and accessibility of music and may exclude many children, by implying that their own culture is not valued. Similarly, forms of dance (such as ballet), certain forms of art (such as oil paintings), certain literature (such as nineteenth-century novels), certain poetry (such as Elizabethan love sonnets) all have the status of high as opposed to popular culture.

Using television to explore attitudes

Using a theme about television can enable us to discuss with them the programmes children watch. An initial classroom survey of popular programmes may indicate that children like 'soaps', *East-Enders*, for example. The way in which these soaps are written about can be considered by looking at a range of newspapers and magazines. Similarly, children can look at how such programmes are advertised and promoted. Children can be encouraged to write advertisements extolling the virtues of their favourite soap, reflecting on the image which they want to promote. They can think about the way the different groups in Figure 2.2 react to this soap. It is quite likely that some schools will not regard such programmes positively. Children may also notice that some newspapers are culturally biased against soaps. Other forms of the arts may be more highly recommended. This can then lead on to the issue of aesthetics and critical evaluation. Older classes may wish to consider the differences between *evaluation* and *bias*. Making videos for themselves sharpens children's critical faculties as they have to make clear choices about the content and the format of what they are trying to communicate. Projects which consider critical evaluation as a challenge can also do this, such as what makes one old master painting more important, both in monetary and status terms, than another? Can children find objective criteria that can be applied so that they are aware of when subjective judgements take over? These are sophisticated arguments which we can begin to offer children during their primary schooling.

As television is watched with increasing frequency at an earlier and earlier age it has a very powerful socializing role, particularly affecting the development of attitudes towards race and gender (Milner 1983; Browne and France 1986). Using television is a powerful way for us to open up an exploration of children's ideas and feelings and challenge prevailing views. Television should be watched 'actively' and its contents and effects discussed. Experiences gained from television are given an emotional framework when children are able to share their feelings with family members (Miller 1992) or with teachers. For children to make sense of complex and potentially challenging images, they need time to discuss their concerns and explore ideas. Schools take on this role by giving children a chance to reflect on and explore feelings engendered by the programmes they see both at school and at home.

Using televisual images

In Cameo 3 the children's enjoyment of television provides a motivation to explore areas of the curriculum in a meaningful way. The children needed to evaluate critically videos of some of the *EastEnders* episodes, to analyse what was presented and the manner of its presentation. Deeper understanding of the medium was gained and examined in relation to their own feelings, both about the characters directly, and about the children's inner selves, through empathy with the roles. The world of popular culture was included within the world of school, avoiding an 'us' and 'them' attitude in children, which could easily have resulted in disaffection.

Exploring unpleasant images

The images we all see on television and in newspapers can be of a very violent nature. Analysis of such images presented to young children gives little evidence of the 'innocent and timeless wonder of childhood' recalled by Rothenstein (1986) which inspired his drawings. Learning through the senses which draws upon pleasurable experience is vital in developing sensitivity and critical awareness. Televisual images are probably the most prevalent source of imagery which children will experience. These images will shape and mould a child's experience of the world. As teachers, we must help children to sort out the visual imagery that they experience, so that we can guide them towards appropriate models, in the same way that we carefully select the items on the interest tables, because they reflect colours, shapes or patterns which may inspire learning. Where pleasant images are shown on television (for example, programmes about natural history) they may well be lost in a maze of successive violent images. It is partly the sheer volume of images that generate the problem; the senses are simply bombarded. I can remember as a child going to see a film and coming out of the cinema still savouring the enjoyable moments of the film and going over the scenes again as I walked home. It was a while before those images were replaced by new ones, and so the emotional quality of the images had time to register in the brain and form permanent memories. Schools can help children to make sense of all the visual messages they are getting, help them to be selective viewers and help them to analyse the pleasant and the unpleasant images they see, so that they have a range of inspirational images to use as a source of creative ideas.

Using discussion and display – the classroom context

'Freeze framing', 'rewinding' and 'replaying' images gives children a chance to talk about their feelings. The class discussion over D-Day and the reality of war helped children to understand some of the underlying realities of the everyday images of violence. Discussion allows ideas and images to be brought to the forefront. Displays should sometimes feature some of the less pleasant images as well as the pleasant, for example the D-Day theme featured a display of newspaper cuttings from a variety of newspapers. This in turn sparked further discussion about the 'facts' and the way in which they were represented. Other issues such as bullying, urban problems or the way that children are portrayed can be treated in a similar way. A salutary experience is to cut out all the pictures and stories about children from five newspapers for a week and analyse the content and images presented. All these examples will help children's aesthetic development, by enabling them to be critical of the forms of representation presented to them.

Key considerations for assessment

An action plan made as a result of teachers completing the following checklist will help to ensure that creative experiences are offered to all children.

The child

- Does the child demonstrate an appreciation of the needs of others in creative work, in discussion and in tackling problems?
- How far does the child share and work willingly in a cooperative and/or collaborative way?
- Can the child express his/her feelings through a variety of media and in a variety of ways?
- Do these expressions indicate an awareness and empathy for different viewpoints, backgrounds, interpretations and representations?
- Is there evidence of any narrowness of outlook which might benefit from a wider range of experience?

The teacher

As well as monitoring the context you will need to monitor your teaching styles and approaches closely and reflect upon your practice.

- Are you favouring any section of the class by paying more attention to one cultural approach to creativity over another?
- Are you providing full opportunities for extending children with a range of individual special needs?
- Are you able to create a classroom climate which promotes a

positive attitude to a diversity of approach and interpretation of creative ideas and expression?

The context

Assessing equal opportunities and creativity in the curriculum means paying particular attention to the resources and activities provided in order to eliminate bias as much as possible. The strategies in the next section provide a useful guide for checking this.

Strategies for change

Look at your resources and activities to discern any cultural bias.

Art

- Check the appropriate representation of non-Western and black artists when looking at the work of artists.
- Explore non-European techniques such as batik and show how designs have travelled, for example paisley.
- Value religious and cultural viewpoints, such as those concerned with the representation of the human form.
- Use children's perceptions of themselves through self-portraits, their homes, families and friends.
- Look at the role played by craftsmen and women and the mass production of artefacts.

Music, dance, movement and literacy

- Check the appropriate representation of non-European and black musicians, choreographers and writers.
- Explore non-European and black styles of dance and musical expression.
- Explore the cultural tradition of oral storytelling, valuing it equally with the written form.
- Value religious customs with regard to music and dance.
- Be aware of the cultural values transmitted through literature.
- Use children's perceptions to explore their feelings through music, dance, movement and language.
- Explore the work of writers, poets and musicians from different social classes.

- Consider the portrayal of different social classes in literature and music.
- Use learning diaries as a way of getting children to record feelings about subject areas, likes and dislikes. These may indicate cultural or gender perceptions which can be explored further.

Drama

- Sensitively explore how children feel about aspects of their identity and culture.
- Explore roles such as worker and manager, shop assistant and owner of a chain of supermarkets, farmer and landowner, in order to develop different perspectives.
- Use historical themes such as industrialization through role play where children can explore perceptions. *Bright Ideas History Projects* (Beetlestone 1993) suggests a scenario on the coming of the railway.

RE

- Check that a range of faiths are being explored.
- Ensure that issues of similarity and difference between faiths are being identified and discussed.

Maths/science

- Consider the appropriate representation of non-European ideas and perspectives (consider where our number system originated!).
- Check that sufficient reference is made to the way in which ideas and techniques travel across cultures, such as patterns and systems of numbering.
- Consider the importance of maths/science to local industry, commerce and leisure.
- Consider the way inventions have affected people in different social situations.

IT

- Check that software gives a balance of images and that black children and girls are represented positively.
- Check cross-cultural implications.

Geography, history and technology

- Check the appropriate representation of non-European countries and of black historical figures, of non-English interpretations of history and non-European and black examples of technology and innovation.
- Consider the underrepresentation of differing religious, cultural and social perspectives that underlie study of other cultures, times and technologies.
- Explore the way the environment is affected by technological change in different countries.
- Consider some of these in a historical context, with regard to geographical regions and how different groups are affected.

Areas to consider for gender bias

Monitor:

- how time is used for dealing equitably with boys and girls;
- the range of experiences being offered to boys and girls;
- single-sex grouping;
- fiction and non-fiction for gender bias – Hughes (1991: 39) has a good checklist for reading materials;
- portrayal of different sexes in displays;
- appropriate balance of themes covered;
- role models used;
- the hidden curriculum;
- how gendered language is used;
- how attention is apportioned to boys and girls;
- equity of assessment procedures;
- the school power structure;
- classroom organization to meet the needs of both girls and boys;
- resource provision and gender suitability;
- children's responses to activities and to each other.

Absence of time is understandable but not a good excuse!
Further suggestions for broadening cultural perspectives across National Curriculum subjects can be found in *Equality Assurance for Schools* (Runnymede Trust 1993). Although the National Curriculum encourages some study about non-European areas in geography, history, English, art and music it essen-

tially has an ethnocentric bias. It needs supplementing and extending (Epstein 1993). Because the most fruitful areas for exploring anti-racism occur in the foundation areas of the curriculum we may be tempted to see it as less important than 'basic skills' teaching; and, of course, it has no statutory directive. Perhaps, more importantly, time is very precious and in short supply. Crucial throughout any teaching in this area remains the teacher's commitment to valuing diversity and to transmitting appropriate values to learners. This means taking on board sometimes uncomfortable and controversial aspects of cultural perspectives. This undoubtedly means looking at the wider political, social and economic contexts, as the D-Day scenario so vividly revealed.

Summary

The National Curriculum is a curriculum for *all* children. Each child is entitled to achieve the most from his or her learning in terms of creativity. Drawing on children's ideas through the expressive arts has been shown to be one way of ensuring that individual needs are met; some strategies have been considered. Children become increasingly confident and independent if they feel their particular experiences are represented in the classroom. Thus, as teachers, we must consider the needs of each child and use a wide variety of tasks and approaches. Linking areas of the curriculum together thematically is one way of maximizing time and energy. It is also important that we are aware of our own attitudes to equity and the way in which the context of social pressures can influence learning. Suggestions have been made for working with parents and the media, for example, in order to provide a way of exploring the creative energies of all children. They can all be creative if we, as teachers, consider their individual and collective needs.

Chapter 3 will now explore the question of whether the creative *process* or the creative *product* has most importance, by looking at the *productivity* strand of creativity.

3

'He just keeps knocking things down!'

The creative process and the product

Cameo I

Tom, a 7-year-old, has spent a lot of time with his teacher, who has tried to get him to be less aggressive and more motivated to learn. She is gratified when he spends one morning building a variety of Lego towers. She shows her delight by praising his efforts and hopes that he will go on to produce more inventive buildings. However, instead he chooses to knock them down. All subsequent building is followed by towers of Lego being noisily pushed to the ground. Tom's delight, unlike his teacher's, seems to be in the destruction not the construction of the buildings. He does not appear to be creatively employed. His teacher's solution is to stop Tom from using the Lego and to give him 'tidier' tasks.

Cameo 2

Fay, aged 5, is fascinated by the musical note sheets which accompany her toy piano. She asks a lot of questions about how the notes on the sheet can be played on the piano. She begins to see the relationship between the printed notes and the sounds produced. After repeated attempts at the nursery rhyme sheets she begins to write music herself. Many hours are spent subsequently writing little tunes, many of which she does not try to play, but some of which she sings. For several months afterwards she writes tunes and then, just as suddenly, she stops.

Cameo 3

Andrew, aged 9, after watching Wallace and Grommit on television, finds some black and white plasticine and proceeds to model Shaun the sheep. He spends some hours working on various versions, experimenting with the shape of the head, carefully constructing the eyes, trying out ways of creating the wool texture and having some difficulty with the legs. He finds it hard to get the legs to be sufficiently thin and yet strong enough to bear the animal's weight. During the process he checks several pictures of Shaun which he has on a box of Wallace and Grommit crackers. He finally produces a model of Shaun. It is universally admired and, indeed, Andrew seems pleased with it. However within a short space of time he destroys the model. In his mind it was not quite right. He is aware that he needs different materials in order to achieve the image that he has in his mind.

Cameo 4

Stella is very pleased with the work her reception class has done this term. The displays reflect her interest in the children's art work. One wall is covered with a 'spring scene' frieze, showing tissue-paper-filled lambs leaping next to more tissue-filled chick outlines. Thirty-five identical egg cards are hanging across the room. Thirty-five identical chick cards which open in a certain way so that the beak moves are set on the table near the door. A row of identical paper baskets sit on the window sill.

Cameo 5

Casim is 6 years old. As he types in his story on the computer, his language skills are developing alongside his technical competence. 'If I press a letter here it will go down here – sometimes you do it so fast that you press the wrong button – see s on skeletons – don't need this [deletes s]. I could write like that [uses forefinger, middle finger], but I write best like this [middle finger].' He counts the lines (six) and then seeks advice on what will happen when he completes the page. He uses the mouse to do *they* from the list at the bottom of the screen – looks for *went* – finds *we* – remarks 'We not went. I'll do that and add *nt*'. It is difficult to move the mouse in the limited space so he does it by hand. 'Sometimes I can write like that' (spreads fingers) 'Do you want to do a g'? He then goes on to enquire 'Why don't teachers have to work?' and becomes involved in a discussion with the classroom assistant about the nature of teachers' work.

Introduction

Much of classroom life sometimes seems to be a challenge to balance conflicting needs – those of the children, who want to engage in a seemingly anarchic process of self-determined behaviour, and those of us as teachers who, like Stella, are trying to ensure evidence of learning. At a time when teachers are increasingly accountable, many children need persuasion to 'produce the goods', to complete activities, the outcomes of which others will understand. We need to reconcile the process–product dilemma. In this chapter, I will examine children's creative processes and consider how we can develop children's aesthetic awareness, enabling learners to use a variety of forms of expression in a context demanding evidence through 'products'.

Creative processes and the child

All the individual children in the cameos could be said to be in almost 'a world of their own'. As Moyles suggests (1989: 70), the process of their learning is clearly more important to them than the product. Tom is happily absorbed with the Lego and quite content to work through his ideas alone. Fay and Andrew are sufficiently occupied to work alone. They seem to have little need of external contact, except perhaps to confirm their own feelings that they are progressing along the lines they have set themselves. Casim makes it quite clear that he is more interested in the process of his typing than getting a finished copy of his story (Figure 3.1). He works alone: the classroom assistant acts as a sounding board for his internal thoughts.

Motivation and involvement with the process

Several things are abundantly clear from the cameo examples. Firstly, the children are mainly self-motivated. They appear to be driven by an internal goal which can almost be seen as a predetermined image. Andrew has an image of the completed model of Shaun the sheep in his mind and he is driven by this to complete the task to *his* satisfaction. Similarly, Fay has an internal image of the kind of music that she wishes to write and how it is done. She keeps going until she is satisfied that she has achieved this internal goal. Tom has decided to explore the way Lego behaves. This could be interpreted as simply destructive or atten-

Figure 3.1 Casim is fascinated by the process involved in typing his story

tion-seeking behaviour, but it may be more than this. He can be seen to be driven by a desire to test how certain hypotheses that he has in his mind match up to reality. Young sees the creative process as involving 'tearing down as well as building up' (1982: 262). As Fryer points out, creativity implies 'the negative as well as the positive. Often what has gone before gets swept away' (1996: 62). We do not find out whether Tom's actions are part of a creative process because he is prevented from using the Lego again, but we can see that he is driven by some internal motivation. Casim was perhaps not initially keen on the task, but he quickly makes it his own by setting himself the task of explaining the process.

If we reflect on Bruner's modes of representation (see Chapter 1), all the children are engaged in an interplay of the enactive and iconic; image and action work together to aid their learning. With Casim and Fay, the symbolic is also brought into play; language, thought and action are all involved. This means that the learning taking place for these children is powerful. Their senses, intellect and emotions are fully engaged. This quality of engagement results in successful learning outcomes. Fay masters the skill of simple composition; Andrew refines his ability to represent accurately an image in 3-D form; Casim masters technical keyboard skills alongside semantic knowledge, and Tom masters technical knowledge about the complexities of space, directional force, gravity and timing.

This learning is in marked contrast to that achieved by the children in Stella's class. The children here have not been self-directed nor motivated to produce the cards, the baskets or the frieze. The enjoyment derived from such tasks may well come from pleasing the teacher, working with their friends in a social group, and the tactile pleasure involved in cutting and pasting. Such pleasures may go some way towards making a socially cohesive class unit, but the creative aspect of their learning has been denied.

One of the difficulties for teachers is in sorting out apparently destructive behaviour like Tom's, which may be essentially creative, from the way in which unmotivated children approach tasks. Some of these difficulties are noted by Fryer in her study of Project 2000 teachers (1996). Unmotivated children may become disruptive in their attempts to avoid the task. They may fail to complete it, filling in the wrong area of the outline, using the wrong colour tissue, getting glue all over the child next to them or simply managing to spend all afternoon gluing one piece of tissue. The teacher has a tendency to reprimand them frequently and, in addition, as they cannot derive much satisfaction from the tasks, their self-esteem is lowered. This leads to a reluctance to investigate further. Thus this behaviour can be seen as different to Tom's because he is motivated to find out more.

Fay, Casim, Tom and Andrew by contrast are all clearly motivated by the *process* of their activities, not the product. This is why Andrew is quite prepared to destroy his final model. It means little to him. It was far more important to him to find out how to develop the sheep's legs and the woolly coat than to produce a finished model. The process was itself the task.

Similarly, Fay's activities centre around the relationship between composing and playing, writing notes and translating those notes into sound. Once she feels she understands and can do it she has no need to continue. Had Tom been allowed to continue, he too would have found the answers to his internal questions and the falling towers would have ceased of their own accord. Casim articulates the process he is going through as if to fix it in his mind, but derives moderate satisfaction from the final production. In his case it is almost as if he has decided to liven up the tediously slow process of producing the typed draft by inventing the fun task of following his own progress.

The motivation involved by the children in these process-orientated tasks is sustained for a considerable period of time. As the process itself takes time, so the motivation is maintained to completion. Skill mastery may be a shorter process: Andrew and Casim are refining skills; their efforts cover a shorter period than Fay's, who is engaged in the mastery of more complex concepts. All the children show characteristics of 'persistence and willingness to work hard in pursuit of their goals' which Fryer notes (1996: 38) are features of highly creative people.

Creative development

All four children are gaining new skills and knowledge about the creative process. Contrast this with Stella's class, whose creative development is unlikely to be enhanced by simply filling in pre-formed shapes. A general guide to the way in which young children's artistic development proceeds is essential both in understanding how their creative potential can be unlocked and enabling us as teachers to understand the process. Lowenfeld and Brittain give four stages of development (1982: 36–7):

- *Scribbling stage*: child is busy exploring the environment through its senses and expresses these through random markings. Exploration of colour, space and 3-D materials. Marks gradually become more continuous and controlled.
- *Pre-schematic*: child expresses experiences real or imagined, with first attempts at representation.
- *Schematic*: child investigates new ways and methods, seeking to find a pattern for his/her relationship with the environment. First use of symbols.
- *Visual realism*: child is aware of groups/social role. Expresses desire to work in a group independent of adults. Drawings become more representational and realistic.

As children go through these stages it is important to recognize that they are learning not just about art but about themselves: they are expressing their inner selves. Children's ideas should be welcomed especially in the scribbling, pre-schematic and schematic stages, where children need to develop confidence in realizing that they have a unique view of the world. As teachers

Suffolk County Council gives five basic modes in which children work:

1 Experimentation and experience of materials and tools (18 months to 18 years)
2 Symbolic interpretation (3 to 7/8 years)
3 Predominantly symbolist approach (from 5 to 12 years)
4 Predominantly analytic approach (from 7/8 years onwards)
5 Analytic approach (from 8/9 years onwards)

Figure 3.2 Developmental stages for art (Suffolk County Council)
Source: Suffolk County Council (1985: 15) in Lancaster (1987).

of young children we must ensure that our priority is to place a positive emphasis on difference and originality so that children avoid thinking that they need to copy. Suffolk County Council's publication offers five basic modes (Figure 3.2).

As with any 'stage' definitions it is important to see these only as approximate but useful guidelines. Children may move very quickly through them and reach stages beyond their age band. They develop at different rates with very individualized patterns. As Lancaster (1987: 13) points out, 'older children and even adults will need to revert to earlier stages as a means of repeating experiences or of strengthening them'. Stages do, however, provide a structure to aid planning. Figure 3.3 gives a helpful outline.

This particular set of guidelines is sufficiently open-ended to allow for potential and is not restrictive. It is very important that no hierarchy is given to particular methods and approaches. It is vital that children are encouraged to recognize the validity of their own perceptions and to develop their own viewpoints within the kind of dimensions already outlined in Chapter 2. Since artistic development, like all other areas of development, is culturally bound it is important for children and teachers to understand the value of a diversity of perspective.

Creation and destruction

Tom and his Lego towers are a clear example of the child interpreting a task at variance from his teacher's wishes. In Fryer's

1 *Scribbling and drawing* (from early infancy)
   - exploration through sensory experience
   - broad physical movements
   - accidental mark-making and freely-made imagery
   - play activities important

2 *Symbolism* (pre-school, infant and early juniors)
   - less apparent random mark-making
   - variations introduced
   - image-making developing more control
   - more considered selection of shapes, forms and colours
   - representational elements more in evidence
   - observation more apparent
   - physical control increasing

3 *Schematic* (mid- to top juniors)
   - increasing emphasis on realism through personal experience
   - more logically-conceived and analysed shapes
   - constructive building of objects and models
   - co-operative group work used increasingly as a working mode
   - work increasingly representational
   - design consciousness awakening
   - increasing interest in technology and analysis

Figure 3.3 Lancaster (NSEAD) stages for art
Source: Lancaster (1987).

study (1996: 62) many teachers were concerned to discourage behaviour which has this effect, even though this is often a characteristic of creative behaviour. It is quite understandable that Tom's teacher reacts by moving Tom away from the Lego. She, like many teachers, may see creation as the opposite to destruction, a view that has been perpetuated by the influential writing of Herbert Read (1943). As teachers we need to channel Tom's energy into a more focused task, such as estimating the area over which the bricks might fall. This could have enhanced his learning in maths, science, technology, language and social development, thus leading to an appropriate outcome for everyone. A glance at Figure 3.4 indicates the amount of learning involved in building with blocks.

Read's view emphasizes a particular aspect of the creative

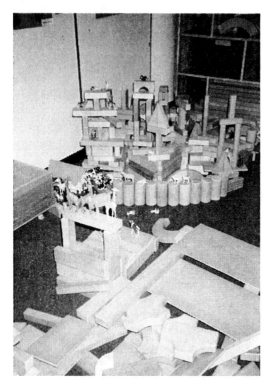

Figure 3.4 The process of building involves demolition and rebuilding

process: it is aesthetically pleasing and always positive. Yet this is only one side of the picture; the opposing forces are drawn together in a cycle of death and regeneration in the holistic framework described in more detail in Chapter 6. Consider the image of creation which nature presents. The growth of plants and animals is accompanied by death. Plants die only to be reborn; animals recreate themselves before dying; the cycle of birth and death is an intertwined process. At times destruction leads to newer, different elements – the forest destroyed by fire gives way to heath. The loss of rural habitats for foxes brings them into urban environments; ladybirds are eaten to provide the next link in the food chain. Destruction and creation can be seen as part of the same process. Tom could be guided into trying to understand these links as well as to master more technical concepts. Out of the destruction of the Lego towers he could eventually gain the ability to build better, more innovative constructions.

When Andrew destroyed his model but did not redo it, his destruction was less obvious than Tom's. It did not impinge on anyone else in the way Tom's falling bricks did. Both Andrew and Fay moved on to the next stage. Andrew decided that he needed more knowledge of different materials and moved on to work with wire as a basis for moulding; Fay decided that her interest lay in lyrics rather than music and she became engrossed for a while writing poems. In both cases the destructive ending of the activity was a positive move after the children had identified their creative needs. They were interpreting creativity as 'an unending living, transforming one' (Barnes 1987: 65), modifying, reflecting and adapting the ideas that they had evolved.

Ownership of the process versus ownership of the product

As noted earlier, all the children in the cameos chose to work alone. They may do this to gain ownership of their learning. Having ownership of the process means far less concern at having ownership of the product. They had control over what they were doing in a way that Stella's class did not, and this was what was important to them. Because Stella had concentrated her children's efforts on producing identical pieces of work the children's individuality was forfeited. They did not feel any particular ownership of the process because it was the same as everyone else's. Most children probably felt attached to the end product and wanted to take the cards and baskets home. Social acceptability and uniformity prevailed and children had something adult-inspired to show, for which they would receive praise from adults.

If we wish to develop children's aesthetic awareness and give them wider experience of creative working, we will need to look closely at ways in which we can develop our teaching role.

Creative processes, products and the teacher

Understanding ownership

Ownership is important to children and teachers alike in the classroom, making a crucial difference to motivation. If children are motivated their self-esteem and self-discipline is enhanced (Edwards and Knight 1994), thus motivating them further. Encouraging children to have a stake in their work means not only sharing the purpose of the task and curriculum with them, but also providing them with a motive (Glasser 1992, 1993). Simply discussing the learning potential of a topic will not answer the children's unspoken question: 'What's in it for me?'

As teachers we can respond to the often heard pleas of children, 'Can I take it home?', 'Can I keep it?' by considering these wishes seriously when planning. The success of home–school reading policies, maths and science packs (Griffiths and Hamilton 1984; Beetlestone 1995a; Mertens and Newland 1996) show that linking home and school through taking work home increases motivation (Figure 3.5). They support the child's ownership of both the learning and the materials, and they win the interest of the parents. Children often need reassurance that they really can take work home, as my work at Culloden Primary on science packs showed (Hancock *et al.* 1994).

Creative outcomes, such as paintings, drawings and models, are often sent home, particularly in the early years. Similar satisfaction is obtained when children take home finished maths

Figure 3.5 Children enjoy the sense of ownership they get from compiling science packs to take home

books, books of their writing and project folders. We can help children to see the ways in which they achieve individual success and give them the tangible proof that adults seem to need – the painting under the arm, the paper crown on the head, the cakes in the school bag or the mustard and cress seeds clutched tightly in a pot in their hand (see Strategies for change section). This sense of satisfaction is so easily obtained, and has been understood by generations of primary teachers and children.

This may be part of the reason why Stella encourages her class to produce identical baskets and cards. She equates creativity with a production line, producing quantities of art and craft outcomes rather than considering the greater educational value of the creative process. She follows a sound principle in making items to take home, but misinterprets it. She could encourage her children to gain much more from these tasks by allowing them some choice over the design and the materials. Nicola's intense concentration on her card (in Chapter 1) indicates just how involved Stella's children could have been with a chance to learn the process of designing and making cards and baskets. As well as enjoying the product, the design and technology curriculum intentions could be more effectively met.

Aesthetic development

As Taylor and Andrews (1993) suggest, children need to be able to work in a way which enables them to discriminate in order to develop critical awareness and appreciate creativity. Stella's approach to art is one in which she supplies children with templates or outlines. These provide children with a ready-made, often stereotypical image of given objects. For example, as King (1978) found, a tree may be outlined as a trunk with a round, woolly top, bearing little relationship to natural forms. For most adults templates act as a kind of shorthand, a symbol which triggers off the desired response, for example the ladies and gents signs on toilet doors. Symbols have a useful function but need to be recognized as such. Providing templates for children makes them potentially reliant and often undermines their confidence in their own efforts. A stereotype of a tree has the same effect on a child as a racial stereotype: as a symbol it provides a shortcut that eliminates the need to investigate and question. It can prevent children from looking closely at the real object, so that they continue to draw trees in the template shape and do not progress beyond this. Templates hinder aesthetic development, as Lancaster (1987) points out, because they fail to give children the necessary chances to explore either their own ideas or the materials.

King (1978) notes that teachers often intervene in children's art outcomes in order to make the product look more recognizable to adults: for example, they think that the children's versions of giraffes and elephants will not look enough like the real animals. Children's art should always be their own because if Stella's frieze had contained the children's interpretation of lambs and chicks based on first-hand experience, it would have:

- provided the children with more detailed understanding of the shape, form, colour and texture of the animals;
- increased the children's technical ability in drawing, painting and forming shapes;
- increased their critical awareness of their own and each other's efforts and outcomes;
- led to a product of higher quality and greater individuality of expression.

She would be helping to develop the four phases of the creative process noted by Abbs (1989) as making, presenting, responding and evaluating.

As teachers we can help to develop children's critical awareness by giving them knowledge and understanding of the processes, a variety of styles and genres, a wide range of materials and techniques, and by developing sensitivity and appropriate attitudes in all of the expressive arts. Developing an awareness of diversity in children is no easy task, but working on close observation of one item, say a daffodil, will produce a variety of drawings which present different interpretations and representations. Encouraging children to value each individual drawing will enable them to see that a variety of perspectives and outcomes are valued, encouraged and equally acceptable.

Children can be encouraged to discuss their feelings about the process and how they evaluate and respond to the variety of outcomes. Good use can be made of their learning diaries (referred to in Chapter 1) to record these feelings. The children's aesthetic development will proceed alongside their technical skills. Displaying work aids critical development (Lancaster 1987; Taylor and Andrews 1993). Being set the task of designing a frieze and helping with the mounting provides young learners with opportunities to:

- make their own decisions about what to display;
- think critically about composition and perspective;
- consider what is aesthetically pleasing to themselves and others.

In such a cooperative task the children see that individual responses are influenced and sometimes changed by the social context and social pressures. Developing sensitivity and using displays are both discussed in the section on Strategies for change.

Good and bad taste

The creative product is always subjected to some kind of judgement about its worth, what Taylor and Andrews (1993: 16) call 'the dynamic interaction between the work and those who engage in it'. The question of taste arises, and some creative outputs may not always be regarded favourably. An artist may think in an original way (for example, Damien Hirst, who meets all the criteria that define art) yet it can be argued that using dead animals is generally in 'bad taste'. We might have similar qualms about children's writing which, though technically sound and beautifully written, deals with bloodthirsty killing.

Taste is governed by social norms: these change over time. Van Gogh sold none of his paintings in his lifetime, yet today his work is highly prized. Picasso was frequently criticized for his cubist-style paintings, now regarded as major works of art. Taste is often responsible for deciding the monetary value of works of art, such as for old masters, with items perceived to be in 'good taste' commanding high prices. Conversely, items commanding high prices often become items of 'taste', such as the work of Damien Hirst. Monetary value does not necessarily equate with aesthetic value; as teachers we should assist children to discriminate between the two.

Discussion about various aesthetic aspects of works of art helps children to build sets of criteria for appreciating it. Surrounding them with examples of art work and aesthetically pleasing collections, such as stones, coloured bottles and ceramic pots, will help to develop notions of public and personal taste (Lancaster 1987).

A study of the arts provides teachers with a way of giving children 'an appreciative grasp of the growth and tenor of our civilisation' (Calouste Gulbenkian Foundation Report 1982: 21). 'Heightened sensitivity and creative awareness' are crucial to aesthetic development (Gentle 1985: 113) and will be encouraged by art, craft and design activities allowing children to appreciate the 'content, form, process and mood' of the work (Taylor and Andrews 1993: 25).

Written and expressed artistic forms

When Fay in Cameo 3 was playing tunes she was both composing and performing. Her interest in the former proved greater than the latter and she went on to consider lyrics and poetry. Had her interest been in performing it is likely that she would have tried out her performing skills on other instruments. Some children may show an equal interest in both areas of music, but skills may be differentially acquired in written compositions and in performance. Though most artists would be proficient in both skills, it is possible to have strengths predominant in one area: many highly competent musical performers are not necessarily good composers.

The written form of ballet, choreography, is similar, for while choreographers are invariably dancers, dancers are not necessarily choreographers. Distinctions exist between acting and writing drama; the writer of prose/poetry and the oral performer; the sculptor and the sculpture critic. The written form involves a more solitary process. The expressed form gains an immediate response and suits children who readily seek, and respond to, an audience. Nicola (Cameo 1, Chapter 1) is very interested in the design of her card and its layout and shows an interest in the forms of art rather than the end product. Similarly, Andrew's interest is in the technical aspects of animating figures rather than performing with them.

Clearly as teachers we need to cater for both aspects of artistic development. Children who are drawn to performing may be more extrovert in personality. Taylor and Andrews (1993: 64) devote several pages to a discussion of Read's views on the introvert and extrovert personality in relation to responses to art, and this book is recommended for further reading. Performers draw on an inner world to support their performance and they retreat into this by taking on a role. Sometimes actors become so immersed in a role that they can be unaware of themselves. Musical performers can become equally transformed by their emotional and technical responses to the music. If a number and range of opportunities are provided for children to engage in role play they will be greatly aided in their development of performance skills. Drama, opportunities for reading aloud, for oral retelling of stories, for playing instruments and for discussion will all increase the skills and confidence needed for performing roles.

The written forms of the expressive arts tend to be undertaken alone and therefore often appeal to the more introvert personality. Writing and painting can be very private skills and are not always capable of being shared. We need to provide opportunities for contemplation and for quiet, independent activity with a sense of privacy. For some children this may lead them to destroy their work rather than have it shared and thus evaluated. Like many writers and artists they may suffer intensely from low self-esteem, becoming both immersed and frustrated in their search for the ability to re-create and represent their inner vision.

As teachers we will begin to see the quality of the process by making time to observe children, to listen to them and to make detailed notes such as those illustrated by the cameos. We may need to suspend judgement for the moment so that we do not immediately see the destruction of work as a negative action. In such situations we may need to look carefully to see the pattern of a child's behaviour. Tom's actions, for example, need sensitive guidance. Regular child observations will help to build up profiles of the ways in which children tackle the creative learning process. Even though it appears that society at large favours the product over the process, teachers need to remain aware of promoting the creative process at every opportunity.

The context for creative processes

Outside pressures

Assessment, timetabling, pressures for pencil and paper tasks and supporting the school ethos can sometimes appear to be at odds with teachers' individual aims, but goals can be reached by a number of means, as the following section indicates.

Providing evidence of learning

Producing evidence of assessed learning is a requirement of the legislated curriculum. This may lead to an increase in the use of children's written work as 'hard' evidence – discussion or play are more challenging to record. Photographing children's activities and experiences is a useful technique. Photographs can record a sequence of events or the way children set up a task, as well as detailing progress and completion. This way of recording is particularly useful for science, maths and technology, allowing teachers the freedom to follow more investigative and problem-solving approaches and still achieve a recorded outcome. Parents love to see photographs of their children and often find a discussion about their child's progress much more helpful when they have photographs to provide the information. Photographic displays, with accompanying explanations, reassure other staff, head teachers, governors and inspectors that the requirements of the curriculum are being met in imaginative ways which extend learning beyond the bare outline of statutory curriculum guidelines.

Art is perhaps better timetabled as an integrated subject alongside others. Working within themes, as discussed in Chapter 1, creates time and opportunities for art throughout the week. The number of minutes and hours in which art was covered during that week can still be noted but there will still be time for ongoing processes to be explored. Paintings and models can be allowed to evolve over time.

Most areas of the curriculum at times require large spaces to develop certain aspects, such as large scale model making. This space is an irregular but continuing need and allows for a wider range of activities and approaches. It can be programmed into the timetable, using either hall, corridor, or outside areas, or by sharing space with colleagues.

As teachers we can develop new ideas and ways of working which will benefit the school while still supporting the current ethos and approach to learning. We can adapt and respond to change by working in collaboration with colleagues on school improvements. An awareness of the benefits to be derived by children through the *process* of their activities as well as the end results will give us the ability to articulate these benefits and to use school displays and staff meetings to promote quality examples of children learning.

Key considerations for assessment

The following checklist will help to ensure that the creative process is fostered.

The child

- What evidence do children show of being able to develop their own ideas in an individual way?
- Do children show an awareness of and interest in the process of a task?
- Are children able to contribute effectively to discussions, for example about solving a problem or interpreting events, showing an interest in the process?

The teacher

- Are opportunities provided for children to feel an ownership of their learning tasks?
- Are a variety of teaching styles and techniques used in order to develop individual patterns of creativity?
- Are children encouraged to discuss and share their ideas/ learning?
- Is time allowed for children to develop their ideas, to experiment and modify?

The context

- Does the classroom/school have examples of individual and group work which reflects children's own ideas?
- Are there examples of process displayed, such as photos of the process of a scientific experiment, drawings of the process of designing and building a model?
- Are these well labelled so that parents, governors, staff and children are aware of the importance of process?

Strategies for change

Increase possibilities for ownership of activities:

- Make more models – use technology sessions to create individual items that are of use to the individual, for example storage containers for things children like to collect.

- Use art more – widen the range of materials and techniques, such as dyeing and batik, clay and photography, using these for children to make individualized presents for family and friends.
- Use IT more – design plans, and ways of recording data which children can use to store their own information. Send printouts home.
- Set more problem-solving activities – use problems children have suggested as a basis, or classroom/playground problems that affect them all.
- Make more games – let children use maths to design and make games that they can play at home.
- Make more books – poetry, plays, stories, – make pocket-sized versions to go home.
- Make more music – make simple instruments, encourage composition and write/print these out so that songs and music can go home.
- Cook on a regular basis – all the organization, management, cooking process and ingredients involved in cooking provide enough opportunities to cover the whole curriculum several times over. Food provides a topic for life. Cook things that children can take home and teach cooking skills that they can use to help at home – always appreciated by parents!
- Grow more plants – like cooking, growth is a subject for life. Grow seeds, bulbs, take cuttings, propagate and let the children do this individually.
- Take photographs of children undertaking activities in all curriculum areas – sometimes get a second set printed cheaply so children can have copies of their own activities.
- Make videos, of children by children which can be borrowed to share at home.
- Surround the classroom with displays of individual work – photos of the children, self-portraits in words and pictures. Celebrate individual success with selected examples across the curriculum. Use their names, their languages, their work, their ideas. Children's stake in the classroom will then be obvious!

Developing sensitivity

Provide a structure which supports aesthetic awareness and helps children to analyse and value creative processes:

- Look at paintings by famous artists. Can you guess the painter's mood? How do we know? What thoughts and feelings are invoked from looking at a variety of pictures/scenes? How do we feel about particular sculptures or models? Do we feel differently looking at them first-hand in a gallery or second-hand via a postcard or picture? Why?
- Consider pieces of music. What do you think was the composer's frame of mind? What might have caused it? What feelings are invoked by different pieces of music?
- Consider well known television characters and scenes. Why did the characters act that way? How might they have felt?
- Give children examples of well known scenes, such as their school at the weekend. Set up an imagined event – what would happen next?
- Change story lines to invent new plots/endings.
- Look at pictures of historical events/characters. How did they feel? Why do we think that?
- Focus on defining problems, for example a picture of a child alone in the playground. Why? What is the problem? How do we know?

Activities similar to these will enable children to increase their skills in relation to developing empathy, understanding different viewpoints, challenging stereotypes, enlarging experience, considering clues and strategies used to make judgements, greater understanding of what qualities are involved in personal preference and the development of criteria for judging quality.

Using display to enhance the creative process

Use displays to:
- inform teaching and learning and provide children with further information;
- show that children's work is valued and enhance individual self-esteem;
- provide an audience for work to be viewed critically, developing the skills needed for aesthetic appreciation;

- provide examples of aesthetically pleasing arrangements of images and artefacts;
- enable interaction so children can learn through enactive as well as iconic and symbolic modes, promoting a feeling of ownership of the displays;
- provide chances for children to do their own displays, increasing a feeling of ownership and aesthetic discrimination;
- reflect a wide variety of styles and images presenting a culturally diverse society, and promoting positive attitudes towards diversity.

Summary

When children are creating they behave as artists. The creation of an end product is often more desired by the audience than the artist. For example the finished painting is admired by those who view it, though artists may have valued the process more, because of their investment in time, energy, intellect and emotion. The process provides the learning experience, but it is the product which gives pleasure to others and is the shared outcome of the artist's work. As teachers we have a difficult role to play in balancing these two needs. On the one hand, we need to foster the process as part of each individual child's personal experience. On the other hand, we have to decide when a product may be needed. Products belong to a wider world. Society may emphasize the value of the product in whatever form, largely because there is something to be seen and the process is often unwitnessed. Less obvious may be the value, especially to children, of the process in terms of individual learning. Since this is a primary focus for education, highlighting the process in the classroom is desirable.

The way in which *imagination* acts as a key element of productivity is discussed in the next chapter.

4

'I don't know if she's naughty or just a nonconformist'

Creativity and the imagination

Cameo 1

Seven-year-old Ellie is writing about oranges: 'My orange is round and orange and the juice is sweet. It smells orangey.' Jodie writes: 'The juice of the orange is nice. You can use it to dye things orange. It stained my T-shirt and my Mum couldn't get it out.'

Cameo 2

David, 13 years old, is asked what he thinks creative people are like. 'Someone who makes things with their hands, creating things, building something and knowing what it would be no matter what the materials are. Something is built that everyone can see.' He describes art as 'A different way of creating, using paper – artists are more quiet people, they keep things to themselves.' Janet, his teacher, expresses her view: 'Creative children are confident, enthusiastic, motivated, full of ideas, capable of self-expression; the type of children who will use any resource available to express an idea, responding imaginatively irrespective of level of skill. They approach activities in a free unpredictable way, often producing something different to what the teacher had in mind.'

Cameo 3

A Year 1 class begin their topic on citrus fruits by looking at a clementine. They spend a morning looking at the external features, hypothesizing about what it will look like inside, the number of pips and segments it may have. This elicits a number of imaginative responses, such as shown by the comments in Figure 1.5. Art work is then used to enable the children to have a closer understanding of citrus fruits through examining 'citrus colours' (Figure 4.2). The children's imagination becomes fired with ideas about these colours; over the next few weeks they not only use them in the classroom for colour mixing, to paint, to print and to use strips of orange, lime green and yellow paper to weave, they begin to bring in items from home in these colours which they have collected, such as sweet wrappers, jelly boxes and pieces of material.

Introduction

Imagination is a driving force behind creativity and the use of imagination can lead children to make unusual connections. As the comments in Cameo 2 indicate, creativity often occurs when children express their imagination in a way that the teacher is not expecting. There can thus be a fine line between creativity and deviance. As Fryer notes, this can lead some teachers to finding creative pupils quite worrying (1996: 57). However, her study indicates that British teachers now seem to be more willing to encourage creativity in spite of these worries. This contrasts with teachers in earlier studies, such as Eriksson's in 1970 (Fryer 1996: 62).

In this chapter we shall look at how children use imagination, the links with play and the way in which teachers can support imaginative development within the context of the National Curriculum. Looking first at children, we can see the importance of imagination to the creative process.

Imagination and the child

How does imagination affect a child's response? In Cameo 1, Ellie's response indicates that she has built up some ideas about the taste, colour and smell of an orange based on her experience. She is able to retain this image, and demonstrates this by being able to write about it. Jodie, on the other hand, has linked together ideas about the orange through impressions which have come from different sources. She has put them together in an original way in order to build up a more complex picture.

Warnock (1976: 16) suggests that imagination is about 'simple impressions which came originally from a different time' joining together to form a complex impression. Two unlinked impressions have been joined together in Jodie's imagination. Her writing then takes on a more imaginative quality than Ellie's. Warnock also says that there 'is a sense in which the imagination is creative, in that it can construct what it likes out of the elements at its disposal' (p. 16). Janet, the teacher in Cameo 2, seems to echo this with the ideas that 'any resource available' will be used by a creative child. In Warnock's view, concepts are acquired through an interaction between received knowledge and inner perceptions. It is the imagination which allows us to make the bridge between 'mere sensation and intelligible thought' (p. 34).

Woods links imagination to creativity and innovation, identifying creativity as having four major components: innovation, ownership, control and relevance (1995: 1). Aspects of these four are referred to throughout this book. Egan and Nadaner (1988: x) are keen to transfer definitions of imagination away from the realms of mere 'fantasy and escape', because they see undue emphasis on these elements as trivializing the importance of the imagination to education. They see imagination as being 'diverse' and note that it has elements which can be used for good or bad purposes. Imagination is a tool which children need to learn to use in a socially constructive manner so that they are less inclined to spoil each other's games, tell tales or hurt each other.

Imagination is related to the expression of feeling and helps to provide an outlet for the subconscious mind, giving a release for otherwise unexpressed feelings, particularly fears and worries, necessary for children's emotional well-being. These worries may be released through dreams (Mallon 1989). If feelings are bottled up they are likely to either repress the individual, which can lead to frustration and low self-esteem, or lead the individual suddenly to release their feelings in uncontrolled and potentially antisocial ways. Thus a 'naughty' child may be one who has not been able to find a more appropriate way of expressing feelings. Sensitive children who feel deeply may have more emotions to express than less sensitive children, hence their use of the imagination to create new and diverse outlets.

Creativity and play

If creativity is about expressing inner ideas, feelings and emotions then it is also about children's play – the normal way in which the young will express their ideas. The variety of forms of play gives children scope to develop their skills and understanding about a wide range of learning such as language and mathematics. Play enables children to explore materials such as sand or paint in order to discover the qualities of texture, colour, form and structure (Moyles 1989). Taylor and Andrews (1993: 53) discuss Read's thesis that the 'arts grow naturally out of play'. Play allows children to explore their emotions by being 'in role' in their imagination. When free from adult constraints, play allows children the chance to:

- participate in their own way;
- interpret tasks in a personal manner;
- let them try out imaginative routes without fear of limitations.

In this way children come to understand themselves in the way they react to the things that interest them and to the consequences of their flights of fancy. They also come to understand the world around them and their place within it.

Play is thus vital in establishing a child's confidence and positive self-image because children respond to their own ideas. The value of play is well known to teachers of nursery and infant children. However, from my limited research I believe that access to play has lessened in the infant school as a result of the legislated curriculum (Beetlestone 1995b). The class in Cameo 3 had access to an imaginative play area and a classroom shop providing opportunities for role play. The children had time within the timetable to express ideas and for spontaneous play, through which they could demonstrate some of their understanding about the concept of 'citrus'. The teacher understood play fully and could therefore utilize it properly (Gentle 1985).

Play also helps children to bridge the gap between fantasy and reality. Imagination often takes us into the realm of fantasy. In role play children can try out new versions of their characters. For example, if they are shy and always fantasize about being in the limelight, then they can adopt starring roles in their play. Through play they can act out fantasies about people and places and come to an understanding of real life consequences and practicalities. Nowhere is this perhaps more obvious than in the playing-out of violent scenes. Fantasy play about wars, shooting or attacking people should be given time by teachers to be played out, so that the children's creative energies are directed less towards violence and more towards trying to visualize the consequences. We can use play in this way to help children to understand that violence imitated from the television does have consequences which they may be unaware of. We can use play as a bridge between the world of the imagination and the world of reality. Imagination can enhance creativity, but it will be unproductive if it is not channelled in positive directions. Much disruptive behaviour stems from a lack of opportunity to play out these fantasies (Goldstein 1994). As teachers we have an important job to do in focusing the imaginative energies of our children in order to maximize learning.

While, as teachers, we can give every chance for children to be imaginative, we need to be aware that some children are more prone to adopting a fantasy life than others. These are the children who daydream, who seem to spend a lot of time imagining themselves as real life or imaginary characters and who seem happiest in a fantasy world. Imagination can project children into a dream-like world, the world of escape which Egan and Nadaner note detracts from the more creative forces of imagination (1988: x). Such escapes can become addictive because they are very pleasurable; they may, in some children, indicate deep-rooted unhappiness. Such children need to be gently guided towards using their considerable imaginative gifts in more directed ways by giving them problems to solve and tasks to achieve.

Very imaginative children may find themselves prey to a large number of fears. As the writing example indicates (Figure 4.1), fear is often about quite trivial things, which nevertheless are very real to the child. Children who feel insecure may be more prone to such imaginings, and an unstable home situation may contribute to such anxieties. Access to videos, television, newspapers and computer games can all create a worrying, frightening and misunderstood context for developing children. Exploring their worries through role play enables children to come to terms with them. As teachers we may also need to be alert to children who become morbidly fascinated with their fears and to channel their imagination in more constructive ways through, for example, discussion and play.

Good opportunities for play will ensure that children do not have to find less acceptable outlets for their actions and reactions by misinterpreting tasks. Play provides a safe opportunity for imaginative risk taking and testing-out of ideas, which can often

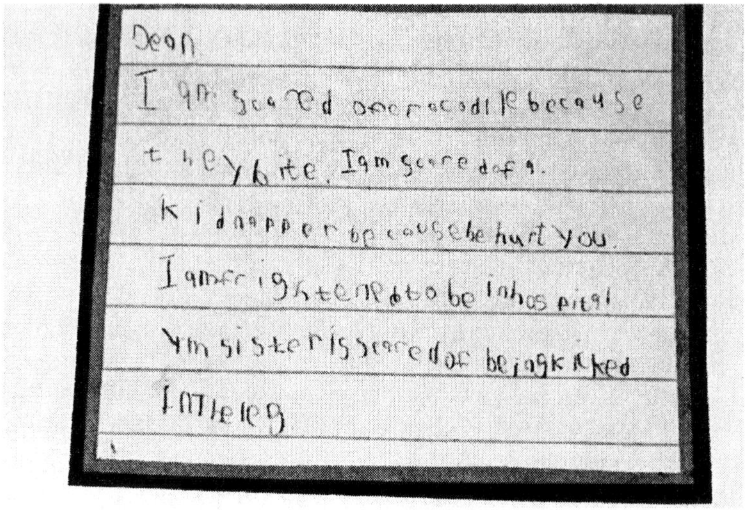

Figure 4.1 Children need a creative outlet for their fears

seem to be non-conformist in character. Children like David, in Cameo 2, may be artistic or imaginative people who 'keep things to themselves'. This can often result in stubborn or uncooperative behaviour or an unwillingness to share. Since such children may become immersed in their inner, personal world they may begin to find it difficult to communicate, or wish only to communicate with like-minded people. In extreme cases they parallel those artists who cut themselves off from the world in order to work with fellow artists, for example the Bloomsbury Group of writers, the Cornish School of painters and the Pre-Raphaelites. This partly accounts for the public perception of the artist as being somewhat non-conformist. Children who follow this pattern may rarely conform to the norms of the class social group but tend to follow their individual courses through life. A study of play helps to illuminate the reasons why children adopt such non-conformist patterns. For more detailed discussions of research and development about play see Garvey (1977), Bruce (1987, 1991), Moyles (1989) and Hall and Abbott (1991).

There are, of course, challenges for us as teachers which we need to consider in developing more imaginative responses in children.

Imagination, creativity and the teacher

Coping with a large class and trying to deal with the sort of individualistic behaviour sometimes manifested by creative children is a challenge we all recognize. Disruptive, sometimes noisy and demanding behaviour can mean that some children get more than a fair share of space, materials and attention. As teachers we naturally have to consider the needs of all our children, and nonconformist or creative behaviour on the part of a few children can take up a disproportionate amount of time. If creative behaviour is well channelled, it enriches classroom life. It is, therefore, worth taking the effort to find ways of accommodating this. Understanding different ways of thinking can help us as teachers to see the importance of catering for them in a free and flexible way.

Convergent and divergent thinking

Creativity, as mentioned in Chapter 1, can be seen as a form of intelligence. As Barrow (1990) points out, the debate about intelligence is long standing. He cites the work of Ryle (1949) who argued that intelligence does not exist *de facto* but that people choose to act or think intelligently. Similarly, people act and think imaginatively or in a creative way. This view enables us to see potential creativity in every child and every situation and to recognize that imagination can be used to achieve this.

The idea of 'divergent' and 'convergent' thinkers first emerged in the 1960s with the work of Liam Hudson (1966, 1968). He, along with others, such as Guilford (1957) and Torrance (1962, 1963), posited the idea that creative thinking is distinctively different from other aspects of intelligence. Hudson saw the converger as one who performed substantially better at intelligence tests than at open-ended tests; the diverger was the reverse. The diverger was likely to make more imaginative connections than the converger. He used this evidence to explain why so many children at the time were underperforming in intelligence tests. Since then many other reasons have been proffered to explain underachievement, and his work has been largely superseded. However, the notion of different forms of thinking has persisted in de Bono's lateral thinking work (1971) and in Gardner's idea of multiple intelligences (1983).

Guilford (1957: 12) considers that 'it is in divergent thinking that we find the most obvious indications of creativity'. Indeed, it could be argued that all young children start off as divergent and gradually become more convergent as they mature and are socialized into different patterns of response. This would help to explain Gardner's view that there is a loss of creativity in older children (1978: 350). Creativity would seem to be more socially acceptable in the young, partly because it is associated with play. If children are divergent or creative thinkers they are more likely to make imaginative connections which could seem odd to a more conformist thinker. Hence the emergence of a view that imaginative children are non-conformist. Hudson linked the divergent–convergent dichotomy to an arts–science predisposition, with divergers showing a preference for the arts. This again supports the view of the imaginative and artistic child as being divergent and less conventional in approach. Fryer suggests that it may be more useful now to replace these 1960s terms, changing convergent to 'analytical' or 'critical' and divergent to 'generative' (1996: 50). Many teachers may indeed find these new terms more straightforward.

Managing non-conformity

Large classes of children need to operate as a cohesive social group and be governed by certain rules and patterns of behaviour to which children must conform. It is our job as teachers to help set and enforce these rules. Some imaginative children may behave in a way which disrupts the smooth running of the class. The less rigidly the class is structured, the less likelihood there is of potential disruption. This is because greater freedom allows space for the individual to respond appropriately. It is possible to organize for learning so that some space is allowed, yet there is a secure structure (Moyles 1992). The teacher in Cameo 3 has managed to find a way of working which enables imaginative children to thrive, by setting up an imaginative programme of work around the theme of citrus fruits.

The concept of citrus is explored across all areas of the curriculum, giving children a chance to find an area of most meaning to them. The teacher provides a Vygotskyian model of a supportive adult, always knowing where and when the children's learning needs extending (see Chapter 1). She makes good use of art and allows the children freedom to explore their ideas within the structured framework of the limited range of

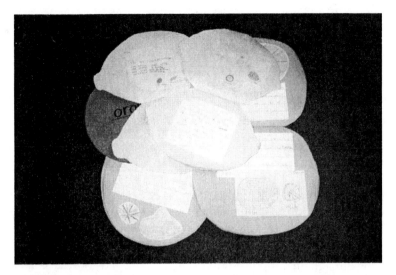

Figure 4.2 Imaginative use of themes can lead to writing with meaning and purpose

citrus colours. The children's self-esteem is high because they feel an ownership of their work. She sets interesting tasks, encourages questions, provides first-hand experiences, gives opportunities for movement and role play, builds confidence by valuing children's contributions and – while keeping the theme within the curriculum framework – still makes learning fun. This is largely because she has the imagination to see that a fairly ordinary discussion about the clementine has the potential for exciting development (Figure 4.2).

Supporting imagination in the classroom

Creative subjects have their own discipline, and although practical work requires space, time and certain materials which could be considered messy, it should never become disorganized. Indeed, art can promote self-discipline through the demands of the skills required. Gentle (1985: 73) notes that 'the making of art as a way of creating one's own order is of great importance'. One way of encouraging more control in practical work is by limiting materials or techniques, such as painting using only black and white, or by sketching with pencil or charcoal. This focuses on particular skills (Skinner 1996) and allows the imagination a chance to operate. The concentration required in such focused work is far from messy or chaotic.

Similarly, music can be quiet and calm if care is taken in the management aspects of presenting musical activities. Noise occurs when sounds become disorganized and unwelcome, whereas working with loud sounds is part of musical development. Opportunities to develop discrimination between 'loud' and 'soft' mean that work with instruments, sound or voices can be quiet for much of the time. Listening to pieces of music enables individual children to imagine scenes, to interpret music and respond more personally, with expression, when performing.

In order to develop children's imaginations fully, we will need to make time for reflection. Quiet periods are needed so that children can delve into their subconscious without external distractions. Looking closely at objects or scenes, listening to music and engaging in practical tasks allows the mind to wander and provides imaginative opportunities. Time is needed to discuss and shape these reflections so that these imaginative ideas can enrich curriculum work, for example writing poems or musical compositions.

While some imaginative children may be divergers or non-conformists there are many examples of creative people who have led very conventional lives. Imaginative children may be equally conventional. They are the ones who require little effort to teach because they appear to grasp new ideas easily and are able to embellish each creative subject with the gifts of imagination. Their writing, art work, models and so on are enhanced by these aesthetically pleasing qualities which are all the more appreciated because they conform to the teacher's plans.

In the next section we shall consider how society views imagination.

The context for promoting imaginative behaviours

Social constraints – assessment

The education world lays great emphasis on accountability through assessment. However, the assessment measures used tend to favour the analytical or critical thinker. If undue stress is laid upon assessment, it may lead to some generative thinkers underachieving. Both are equally important and differing approaches to learning should be reflected in assessment processes. The re-emergence of standardized testing, in the form of standard attainment tasks, raises anew the issue of fairness. After only a few years of operation it is clear that some groups of children continue to underachieve. It may be necessary to review our system to explore whether particularly creative children are among those who underperform. We should avoid heavy reliance on testing as a mean of evaluating the way children learn so that the curriculum provides benefits for all children.

Art, sensuality and conformity

Artists are able to feel with, and to use, their senses; they are literally 'in touch' with stimuli focusing on smell, taste and auditory experience as well as on the tactile and visual. Thus art, especially fine art, is a very sensual pursuit (Skinner 1996). People who become involved in the creative process learn about their inner responses, which may include learning about their feelings about sex and sexual identity.

If imaginative people have the 'capacity to respond emotionally and intellectually to sensory experiences' (Brierley 1987: 67) they may also reveal areas of human experience which can be considered socially unacceptable, or areas which some sections of society might seek to suppress. For example, society sees it appropriate for children of the later years of secondary schooling to engage in the study of the naked human form, when it dignifies interest in the human body with a cloak of academic respectability. It would largely be seen as inappropriate for children in their primary years because of adult concerns to protect them from exploitation, but it could be beneficial in helping children to understand confused feelings about their growing bodies. We cannot ignore the reality of the young being aware of such images. For example, if we visit an art gallery with a class of children, how do we avoid them seeing a nude figure? Nor can we ignore the fact that children are surrounded daily and at an early age by exploitative images of the largely female naked body through media representation. Providing a framework where confused ideas can be discussed is, to my mind, a function of creative education.

With an awareness of these aspects of creativity we possess a fuller picture of what it means to be creative. One could argue that it may be in everybody's interests to unleash these feelings and put everyone in tune with their emotions, though this would undoubtedly lead to a less conformist society. If teachers are seen as largely conformist and if schools are the agents of state (Bowles and Gintis 1976) whose job it is to maintain the status quo, then these views are unlikely to change. As teachers we are, however, able to encourage imaginative individuals regardless of whether or not the climate is supportive; we have an important role to play in promoting a more creative society. As we have seen earlier, society needs people with a creative approach in order to tackle the current complex economic, industrial and social situations which prevail. Fryer (1996: 5) suggests: 'To cope with the demands of the future, people will have to be quick thinking, flexible and imaginative.'

Social constraints – the curriculum

The curriculum provides some constraints which would seem to limit teachers from providing for the imaginative exploration of ideas through play and drama. Role play is essential for developing creativity (see Strategies for change section). The legislated curriculum provides some opportunities for play, and the DOCLs document (SCAA 1996) includes suggestions for imaginative development under 'creative development'. As teachers we need to explore every opportunity to provide for imaginative play; particularly we need to find ways of increasing such opportunities for older children. Written work, for example, is enhanced by children using wider and more complex vocabulary and more imagery, and when their stories have a greater understanding of characterization. Many of the teachers in Fryer's study expressed concern at children missing out on imaginative play and the potentially detrimental effect on children's creative development. For example, children need to explore the qualities of 3-D materials through play before they are able to make quality sculptures and models.

Teaching creativity inside and outside the state system

Schools need to adopt an approach which supports creative development otherwise they leave themselves open to the argument that 'conventional education is hostile to creativity' (Hudson

1970: 231). Progressive private schools which encourage the arts may be more congenial to 'independent spirits' than the state system.

This supports an argument for creative, imaginative children being taught in different settings if they are deemed to require many special facilities. Specialist schools, such as ballet or stage schools, may provide better technical support, though this can mean children are restricted at an early age from contact with wider social groups. There is also the chance of being pressured by the competitive atmosphere. State schools can provide the necessary 'cutting edge' which Hudson (1970: 232) sees as sparking the imagination. Let us look at some of the ways that extra facilities can be provided in state schools to increase provision for the majority of children.

If resources are restricted, teachers will always make good use of cheaply available 'found' materials to support activities such as art, craft, technology and mathematics. Where more specialist tutors are required, for example in musical instrument tuition, fine arts and poetry, specialist teachers should continue to be employed on a peripatetic basis. Schools can form local cluster groups to share the cost of this tuition. Some schools have invited authors and illustrators during 'book weeks' or have engaged artists in residence to provide additional sources of inspiration for their children. Local theatre groups, painting circles and craft workshops may all be willing to send some members along to schools to support and enrich class projects.

Many parents and governors may have skills which they are willing to offer on a voluntary basis. Similarly, schools make great use of the specialist facilities provided by local and national museums, galleries and historic houses to promote aesthetic understanding and to widen children's experience of the creative arts from a curriculum basis. Commercial companies and local firms are becoming increasingly involved in sponsorship and may be willing to support school initiatives. For example the trade union, Unison, sponsors the National Youth Jazz Orchestra.

Providing for specialist needs also occurs in after-school clubs, extra classes and sessions when extra time and facilities can be made available. Sweden provides a model of such a fully resourced out-of-school state-provided system. It is in these after-school sessions that additional creative activities take place. Musical instrument tuition is expensive to provide and parents may have to pay towards tuition costs. However, many schools have increased their stocks of instruments in order to provide opportunities for as many children as possible to participate despite difficult financial situations. Future conductors, orchestra leaders, harp soloists, trombone, sitar and steel drum players are awaiting discovery! An entitlement curriculum means providing imaginative chances for *all* children.

Key considerations for assessment

The following checklist will help to ensure that imaginative opportunities are provided.

The child

- Does the child draw upon a wide range of experience to enhance, for example, written work, drawing and modelling?
- Does the child use a good range of vocabulary in order to express ideas?
- Is there evidence of imaginative interpretation, for example through storytelling, drama and writing?
- Does the child enjoy listening to stories, music and the views of others?
- Does the child express ideas confidently and enthusiastically through movement (both in role play and with music)?
- Does the child show an ability to draw upon a variety of ideas, techniques, experiences and resources to interpret and express ideas?

The teacher

- Are ample opportunities given to develop listening skills?
- Are there opportunities for quiet, reflective periods in the day so that children have time to imagine real and fantasy situations and events?
- Are children encouraged to take risks and to test out their ideas?
- Do children feel supported in these initiatives?

The context

- Are the resources provided, such as clay and other natural materials, likely to stimulate the imagination?
- Are areas set aside for potentially messy and noisy creative activities?
- Does the learning environment provide a secure basis for risk taking?
- Are children able to leave out ongoing work so that they can continue with it in a 'workshop' way?

Strategies for change

Imaginative play

Providing for imaginative exploration of ideas through play and drama is essential for developing creativity. Though teachers of the early years generally place emphasis on the development of imaginative play and provide space in the classroom for such areas, children from around 5 or 6 years upwards are often less well provided for.

- Set aside an area of the room which allows children to explore roles, no matter how small that space may be.
- Divide this area off with screens, bookcases or improvised structures, using corrugated card or trellis.
- Include chairs and tables so that children can work within the space – they may be 'counters', 'cafe tables', 'desks in an office'.
- Decide on your aims and objectives for this play, just as you would for any other area of curriculum.
- Make this area a focal point of the theme – for example with a theme of 'travel' set up a travel agents and build the curriculum around it.
- Make the focus of the technology curriculum the design and setting up of the area. Monitor its use and operation.
- Give children the opportunities to take on a variety of roles and perspectives – counter staff, customers, managers, cleaners.
- Allow time for free and individual interpretation as well as setting up some structured tasks – exchanging currency, booking a holiday.

- Follow up work done in these areas by extending ideas in writing, reading and maths sessions, for example writing about holiday experiences, reading accounts of travels and exploring the concepts of money and exchange.
- Follow up these ideas with art work – making posters and window displays; for IT work, recording holiday data; for music, making background tapes for the setting; for geography, thinking about changing climate; and with history, studying how areas have changed.
- Where possible make appropriate costumes – this provides for role play in greater depth, and enables mathematical and technical skills to be used.
- Allow children to suggest ideas and to follow through discussions so that their imaginations are used to help formulate the curriculum.
- Provide for times of quiet and contemplation for the whole class.

Resources to encourage the use of the imagination

- Provide a quiet corner of the room where individual or pairs of children can think, imagine, create and discuss.
- Allow children to interpret their own ideas by giving them materials to use without preconceived ideas.
- Use materials that allow for imaginative use – clay, wood, cardboard boxes, pieces of fabric.
- Provide ample opportunities for different forms of construction and also small world play (farm animals, vehicles, small people).
- Encourage children to dramatize their ideas and play out scenes with a variety of puppets and role play.
- Use props – hats, pieces of fabric, artefacts – to suggest new uses rather than very specific tools or materials, for example a large box can become a house, a car or an aeroplane.

Encouraging sensory awareness

Visual

- 2-D displays of paintings, drawings and prints both by children and other artists
- 3-D displays of sculpture, glass, wood, fabrics and artefacts.

Sense of smell

- For the focus of classroom displays use tables of fruit, flowers, herbs, spices, vegetables and food.
- Encourage children to focus on the smell of paints, art materials and natural materials such as wood when they are working.
- Make lists of descriptive words evoked through smell when teaching topics. (Describing smells is harder than describing visual images and our response to smell is often subconscious.)

Taste

- Set up experiments, for example which flavour can be discerned in assorted crisps? Can children distinguish between makes of cream crackers? Try blindfold tasting to guess the flavour of sweets.
- Have opportunities for cooking and eating. Encourage discussion of the tastes involved.

Sound

- Set up sound tables featuring a variety of objects, such as everyday items or musical instruments both bought and made by the children.
- Play music in the classroom with focused listening times on a regular basis.
- Make the use of tapes and tape recorders part of regular practice.
- Provide opportunities for quiet listening on an individual or paired basis.

Touch

- Provide tactile displays with materials and natural objects, featuring a variety of textures.
- Set up opportunities to handle objects and explore materials manually.

Imaginative teaching through a range of teaching strategies

In order to develop imagination teachers need to increase the range of strategies they are using. The chosen technique should fit the purpose of the activity, and 'fitness for purpose' should be the single important criterion. A balance of styles has been shown to be highly effective (Ofsted 1993a: 32). The following list provides a very useful reminder of the range of strategies that should be used:

- questioning
- observing
- explaining
- discussing
- providing feedback
- modelling
- task matching
- assessing
- diagnosing
- collaborating
- demonstrating
- listening
- organizing
- supporting
- guiding
- being 'in role', for example for drama/story times
- instructing
- giving information.

Summary

When we look at creative behaviour we can see that there is a fine line between creativity and non-conformity. For children this may mean that their imaginative responses may sometimes be at odds with the rest of the class. As teachers we can maximize learning opportunities by encouraging a wide range of potential learning styles and responses for all children. Adopting a range of teaching strategies and providing a fairly flexible framework will enable us to meet more readily a diverse range of needs. This task is easy if the context is made more flexible and if schools carefully consider their resource provision. Imagination is to be welcomed as bringing a delightful freshness and originality of approach to enliven learning for both teachers and children alike.

The question of *originality* in the creative process is addressed more fully in the next chapter.

5

'I'm not creative myself'
Creativity and originality

Cameo 1

Lesley has a lively Year 2 class. Her room has many artefacts
and resources arranged so that there is a feel of a workshop
about it. Children are busy in all areas. Casim is typing a
Funnybones story on the computer; four children are busy
cutting out photos of themselves as babies and toddlers for a
time line, while Stephen is already mounting his photo in a
zigzag book. A line of finished paintings hangs overhead. Four
children are moving busily around the room measuring items
and recording data on their clipboards. Two girls are doing a
survey about school dinners, while two more are closely
observing the tulips in a vase perched rather precariously on
the edge of the table next to the hamster. Six children are
busy marking, cutting and sawing as they make up boxes they
have designed. Sarah is reading quietly in the imaginative play
area. Somewhere amidst all the quietly productive hive of
activity, Lesley is working with a group of children discussing
their writing about foods beneficial to growth. The children all
know what they are doing and Lesley keeps careful notes on
their activities and progress.

Cameo 2

Julia's Year 1 class are enthusiastic about all areas of the
curriculum. She has a particular approach which involves
exploring imaginative ways of recording. Much work is done as
a whole class working in pairs, which Julia finds is a supportive
way of encouraging learning. Some of the children are printing
and then using felt tip pens to draw on images, producing a

range of original and distinctive pictures. Several pairs are collaboratively drawing routes to the local park. Other pairs are trying to imagine what the classroom would look like from the ceiling and are drawing various classroom features. Two pairs of children are working on investigations into preferences following the reading of John Burningham's *Would You Rather?*

Cameo 3

Adrian is 9 years old. He is working on a new design for an aviary for his pet canaries. He shows considerable skill and his design has flair and originality. His graphic work always stands out from the rest of the class, both because of his technical expertise and the inventiveness of his responses to such tasks.

Introduction

This chapter looks at the strand of *originality* and the question of whether being creative always means being original. What do we mean by originality, and is it innate or can it be nurtured? Some teachers see creativity as a rare and original gift which few children possess. They look expectantly for the spark of creative genius. They know they themselves are not creative geniuses, but they are ever hopeful for their pupils. Other teachers, like Lesley in the cameo, see creativity all around them in everyday activities.

In this chapter we shall consider ways of making opportunities for creative development and promoting a supportive classroom climate, just like Lesley and Julia. First let us explore whether creative children are born or made.

Creativity, originality and the child

Creators of something totally new are very rare. Those who invent, create or perform in a totally unique way have technical skills and vision which are quite extraordinary and uncommon. This rarity gives rise to the view that such people are born geniuses. They are seen as being endowed with particular inborn, innate gifts for, say, music or ballet. Shallcross (1981: 2) points out that most studies of creativity have tended to start by looking at the characteristics of highly creative people and thus see creative gifts as being rather sparingly bestowed. Arguing against this view, she suggests 'Creativity is not the exclusive possession of the chosen few . . . creativity exists in all of us . . . in varying degrees', as do 'other kinds of intelligence' (p. 2). We recognize that Adrian in Cameo 3 may be gifted above the average because his talents are so obvious. We may, however, fail to spot potential in others if we are too wedded to the notion of innate endowment.

Far more useful is the view that creativity consists of what is unique to each individual and original to them, rather than what is original to the world – in Shallcross's terms, whether the item is 'new to the person who created it' or whether it is new and 'has not existed before'. The debate is about the 'individuality or commonality of the creative process' (p. 10). Most ideas are recirculated, so we could spend a lifetime trying to find totally new thoughts and means of expression. Instead, let us take the view that every person has creativity to a greater or lesser degree, and all children are capable of rearranging ideas and generating meaning in original ways.

Tiers of creativity and analysing creative response

When considering creativity in schools it is helpful to think of a three-tier system of creativity:

Tier 1

All children have the right and the ability to express their inner thoughts and feelings, to create ideas, products and ways of working which are unique to them. This is the sort of creativity we can see in the busy classrooms of Lesley and Julia, each child working effectively to produce or express themselves in their own way.

Tier 2

Children begin to make unusual and different connections between things; their work has a particular individual style. Reflection and discussion (the process shown in Figure 5.4) produces new answers to problems, imaginative links in written accounts, new ways of visualizing design and so on. For example, an artist may make connections between still life and dead sheep; an architect may combine elements of cottage design with underground station design; a musician may fuse music from different cultures, ages or traditions. Adrian in Cameo 3 is behaving in this way, fusing unconnected elements in his bird cage design which makes his design stand out from the others. It is this element of creativity which is the most useful in terms of social and cultural development. A society is moved on by new connections being made and new ways of approaching tasks. This can also be an extremely satisfying process for individuals as they begin to take imaginative leaps into the unknown.

Tier 3

These connections truly become something new to society and because of the technical expertise and vision involved, reach a level of genius.

Viewed in this way we can see that it is possible for all children to reach the third tier, if given appropriate opportunity. Since children, as a mass, have never had the opportunities to express their ideas and to make connections in Tiers 1 and 2, it is impossible to say whether appropriate nurturing, guidance or modelling for larger numbers of children might more often produce a genius. Most children can produce something unique to them; having achieved this, teachers will go on to develop skills in order to promote the children's second tier of creativity – that of visualizing new possibilities and making new connections. Most teachers believe that creativity can be developed and are committed to doing so (Fryer 1996: 74).

In Cameo 1 ample opportunities are shown for self-expression (Tier 1) within a tightly structured curriculum. For example, Casim, working alone on the computer, has time to muse about the process as well as complete the task. The group cutting out their photos for the time line are able to discuss how they looked and felt as younger children and are able to mount their work individually. The measuring group has a chance to make choices about what they measure: they discuss their ideas and respond to the feelings of the group about the task. Each child in the cameo has the chance to think, to discuss ideas and/or to express themselves in a variety of ways. This accounts for the calm, purposeful atmosphere of the classroom.

Julia's class is larger, and so she has used the idea of peer support to give the children opportunities for discussion and cooperative work. The children's learning is being 'scaffolded' by their peers, so that they are able to learn more through the interaction and support of their partners than they would alone. They have been given tasks which enable them to respond imaginatively. Two of the tasks ask children to make connections and consider diverse viewpoints. By using two contrasting resources and techniques – the printing with paint and the felt-tip pens (Figure 5.1) – she has encouraged the children to consider these connections and to integrate them in an original way. This activity allows

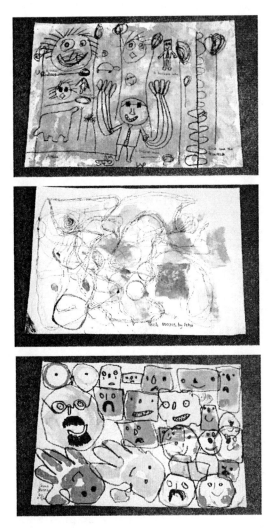

Figure 5.1 Contrasting techniques and materials have been used to create an imaginative response

them to respond as individuals. The task of drawing the route to the park with a partner means that the children are forced to consider each other's experiences and perceptions. As a result of this discussion perceptions are shared: the children learn about what they have noticed and taken in from the experience as well as understanding how very different other perspectives and experiences may be.

Adrian, in Cameo 3, has had his talents recognized and, as a result, he receives a high level of praise and support. His teacher has encouraged him to develop his ideas further by giving him the chance to work them through in a personalized task. His motivation has been engaged because he has a purpose to design, to produce and to modify his work in order to create something both useful to him and aesthetically pleasing. There is plenty of flexibility within technology tasks to allow for individual interpretation. For example 'creating a suitable home for a pet' can meet standardized learning targets at the same time as allowing for personal choice.

Most teachers are well aware of their role in promoting creativity and are aware that they can 'act as catalysts, inspiring and enthusing' (Fryer 1996: 79). Much energy in classrooms is directed to providing what Fryer describes as a 'supportive climate in which creativity can happen or on teaching [creative arts] skills' (p. 88). Teachers need to be aware equally of the necessity to teach problem solving and thinking skills which are vital to creative development (p. 88).

In the next section we look at how teachers can overcome potential constraints in order to develop each child's originality.

Strategies for teaching creativity

It would be naive to think that there are no difficulties facing teachers when they try to set up increased opportunities for creativity. The Project 1000 teachers in Fryer's study (1996) thought that there were six key factors which hindered the development of creativity:

- a constrained environment;
- a home background where child's activities were mostly proscribed;

- teachers encouraging 'quick' work;
- assessment by examination;
- peer group pressure;
- stressing differences between work and play (p. 114).

Eighty-three per cent of teachers in Fryer's study felt that 'the constrained environment' was the most significant. Nevertheless, most teachers find ways of overcoming constraints. Woods (1995: 3) points out that 'creative teachers need choice and the power to make it'. Many teachers do find that they can 'modify the circumstances and increase the range of opportunities' (p. 2). Quite remarkable perseverance has been shown by teachers, and they continue to find strategies to develop creativity in their children. So how do we do this?

Planning for creative teaching

One way is through our approach to planning for teaching and learning. Children learn through interaction with materials and with each other; they see the curriculum within a holistic framework. Effective planners are able to manage classes (regardless of the constraints of large pupil numbers, lack of space and resources) and create a particular and individual style of working environment. Planning is central to effective and creative teaching. The most effective teachers identified in an Ofsted study were those who identified the structure and content of sessions to include carefully thought-through plans for groupings, timings and resources; they also used assessment of pupils' learning to inform planning (Ofsted 1993d: 18). Both Lesley and Julia have considered all these factors in order to maximize opportunities for encouraging children to develop creative and original ideas. Julia has given very careful thought to setting up paired work. Lesley's records on the children have shaped the structure of the present session, those which came before and those coming after. Creative learning and development does not 'just happen'. As Moyles points out (1989: 78), teachers have to 'encourage creativity and artistic expression through providing children with the appropriate techniques and materials'. Figure 5.2 shows a child concentrating on her learning as a result of the activity being thoroughly planned to meet her needs. As teachers we need to plan creative experiences carefully into schemes of work to ensure that progression and development are as evident here as

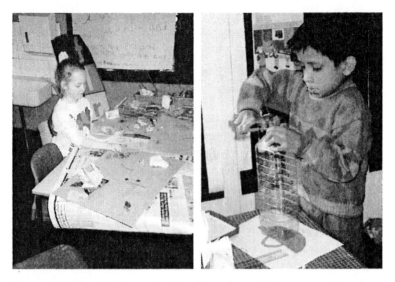

Figure 5.2 All activities need to be planned carefully to ensure learning

in other curriculum areas. Long term planning should focus on the knowledge, skills, attitudes and concepts which are required to develop creative individuals, rather than simply thinking only of what children will *do*.

Planning itself is a creative task. It can be seen as 'writing a play' (Frost 1997: 4). As such it provides teachers with a blank canvas on which to express their originality. How exciting to be able to decide how to present learning – through games, activities, projects, questions to ask, facts to be discovered! How do we want children to learn? by the ablest readers helping others? Do we encourage a musically gifted child to develop a class performance? How do we involve the special experiences of bilingual children? Teachers can retain their own vision of teaching and maintain their creativity through commitment to their learners as creative individuals. The curriculum is there for us to present, for us to divide up into scenes and tableaux to present to our audience – our class.

Dealing with constraints

This sense of excitement can eliminate stress whenever it threatens to affect motivation. Stressed teachers will resist change and want to stick with tried and tested methods. Creative teachers realize that any barriers (internal, external, real or imagined) are removable (see Strategies for change) because they are always seeking to remove obstacles which prevent them exploring new ways of working. The teacher–child conferencing approach much used in reading (Temple *et al.* 1988; Campbell 1995) is one way of helping children to identify barriers to their own learning needs. Teachers can use similar techniques of teacher–teacher conferencing in staff development or inservice sessions to identify where learning barriers exist for them. Reflective journals (see Strategies for change section) can be useful for this purpose.

If teachers are inhibited by the perception that a creative teacher is someone who is 'very good at art' or 'musically gifted', then it will be useful to reconsider this notion. Shallcross (1981: 242) provides a list reproduced in Figure 5.3 against which such insecurities can be assessed. Removing barriers enables a sense of enthusiasm to be generated. Enthusiastic and creative teachers are likely to produce enthusiastic and creative pupils.

Habit
Learned behaviour/conditioning
Assumed expectations of others
Failure to be aware of all the available information
Lack of effort/laziness
Assumed or self-imposed boundaries
Mind set
Rigidity/inflexibility
Fear of failure
Conformity/fear of difference
Fear of ridicule
Reliance on authority
Following the behaviour patterns set by others
Routine
Comfort
Familiarity
Need for order
Superstition
Acceptance of fate, heredity or station in life

Figure 5.3 Internal factors blocking creative thinking
Source: Shallcross (1981).

Sometimes, charisma may appear to be an essential character-istic in developing originality – indeed, most charismatic people are enthusiastic and able to inspire others. However, according to Fryer (1996: 123), the most dominant personality traits shown by creative people are 'persistence, tenacity and commitment'. They keep going long after everyone else has given up! These are char-acteristics which many a hard-working teacher regularly demon-strates.

Finally, many constraints are overcome by teachers successfully encouraging children to solve problems, by teaching thinking skills and by turning constraints into challenging problems, for example 'How can we share six pairs of scissors among nine chil-dren?', or 'How can we make sure that four packs of card last us till the end of term?' Such questions enable children to begin the creative process by making them think, come up with ideas, try them out and so on until they arrive at useful solutions. This is the strand of creativity perhaps the most in need of development. It is this strand which has universal application within any cur-riculum area and thus moves creativity away from the arts to the more logically based subjects. It is worth emphasizing, however, that thinking skills need to be taught.

Training in the use of creative problem solving can give teach-ers useful strategies, for example, by using the approach sug-gested by Shallcross (1981) or by direct analogy (Fryer 1996: 90–9), both outlined below.

Shallcross suggests that problems can be tackled by using a five-stage approach:

1 *Orientation*: why solve the problem? What is the aim?
2 *Preparation*: what information do you have and what more do you need to know?
3 *Ideation*: the process of generating ideas for a solution. Solo brainstorming should be used to stretch thinking. Group brainstorming can then be useful.
4 *Evaluation*: criteria need to be adopted in order to draw up a short list of possible solutions. Ensure that some 'way out' ideas are retained.
5 *Implementation*: what will be the first stage? Who will be involved? What time scale will apply?

It is clear that children will need many opportunities to practise before they become skilled in this way of working.

Fryer's *direct analogy* involves trying to bring together ideas from different fields. In order to make good use of synergy (cooperative energy) you could set up a 'mini-task force', bringing together children with particular skills (such as being very physically adept, articulate, good at calculation, a good listener or being able to draw plans) into a problem-solving group. Collectively they may be able to solve a problem through bringing to bear ideas generated from these different sources of strength.

The role of the teacher in promoting creativity

The ultimate endeavour is for teachers to be able to 'set the creative pattern in which the creativity can flow' (Sisk 1981: vi). Like Lesley and Julia we can provide role models for creativity through enthusiasm, inspiration and attention to a quality environment. As teachers we need to be involved in 'observing, initiating, participating, encouraging, maintaining, extending' (Moyles 1989: 76) – a role that clearly means being aware of the nature of creativity and how to develop it in ourselves. We should see teaching as involving a change from 'a passive acquisition of knowledge' towards activities which help children 'to discover and develop their creative abilities by doing, making and organising' (Kyriacou 1986: 182).

We may need to adopt 'open' attitudes to change, have a positive outlook and be able to use problem solving to free up creative potential. Creative potential is a force which needs to flow. The creative thinking involved in problem solving is about using divergent patterns of thinking, but using convergent thinking in order to apply them effectively. 'The highly skilled creative person uses divergence and convergence equally well' (Shallcross 1981: 70). Lesley demonstrates divergent thinking by planning a wide range of curriculum activities which foster problem solving and individual expression, and she uses convergent skills when deciding when to use them and how to plan them within the constraints of her setting.

Alexander *et al.* (1992: 35) encourage teachers to 'provide learning tasks which will enable children to engage in creative and imaginative thinking and action'. Creativity is seen here in its widest sense, not just as applicable to the creative subjects of the National Curriculum. Julia and Lesley demonstrate just how exciting and satisfying such teaching can be for teachers and children alike. Schooling can only be really effective if the classroom climate is conducive to learning, and if teachers have a clear organization and management role. Having set the scene with the planning and written the script, teachers then take on a stage manager role, deciding on the most original and appropriate way forward. This means taking a non-conventional and original view.

Managing the class – sharing responsibility

The 'stage manager' needs to involve the 'players' so that they have a clearly structured day with daily goals and targets defined. Children need to share both the purpose and inception of the planned activities and be given encouragement to evaluate the results. They are the 'actors in the play' and as such need to understand their roles. If there is a shared framework of class-room discipline and organization in which each individual has a stake, the teacher will be free to manage. As stage manager, the teacher's role is to ensure that the needs of teachers, children, cur-riculum, parents, statutory requirements, staff and governors are met in a balanced way, so that all parties can fully participate and enjoy the 'production' of learning.

Apportioning time for creative thinking

A key management consideration is the provision of sufficient time for children both to develop original ideas and for the cre-ative process. Whether children are involved in typing out their stories on the computer, developing a time line, designing boxes, measuring the hall or working out how their classroom might look from the ceiling, they cannot be hurried. Such activities require the same process – thinking which looks both inward and outward for sources of inspiration. Time is needed to think alone about ideas; to seek key elements, needs and constraints (inward reflection). Time is needed for discussion, reading, observation and experience (outward influences). There then needs to be fur-ther time for reflection (inward) to assimilate the outward influ-ences. The process may be repeated once or several times until initial ideas have been modified into workable plans of action (Figure 5.4).

We can provide more time if we show the ways in which the creative process is, in itself, meeting the needs of the curriculum.

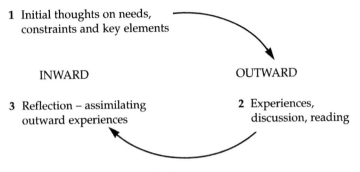

1 Initial thoughts on needs,
   constraints and key elements

INWARD   OUTWARD

3 Reflection – assimilating   2 Experiences,
   outward experiences   discussion, reading

Figure 5.4 The process of reflection

It is integral to effective and creative learning, not a bolt-on acces-
sory. Hence we need to allow enough time within realistic dead-
lines (Ofsted 1993b: 22) to focus on creative thought, and to
ensure that children have clear aims. We will need to monitor
how we are managing our own time and plan this effectively. For
example, how good are we at listening and observing as well as
imparting information? What proportion of time is spent on these
important aspects? Is there a balance? As stage manager, the
teacher will need to deal with the timing and sequence of activities, allowing for individuals to take a full learning role.

Managing adult assistance

The successful teacher develops their role still further, becoming
the 'director', managing all those other adults who are involved
in the learning process. As Woods points out (1995: 8), teachers
have always been very creative in managing other adults to support their teaching. While extra adults in the classroom can be
used to cover some of the mundane tasks, as directors we should
be looking to see if we can deploy such help more effectively. If
helpers are used to support discussion and reflection they will be
giving children the skills needed to develop originality. At the
same time better use is being made of the knowledge and experience which these adults, be they parents, assistants or community
workers, bring to the classroom. We may need to support them by
sharing with them ways of listening to children and supporting
their autonomy, so that they are not tempted to overdirect or to
place undue emphasis on models or templates which might
thwart children's originality. All adults working with children

will need to be aware of how to help them to make the sort of imaginative connections referred to earlier. Good management of adult assistance is highlighted by Ofsted (1993a) and in research by Moyles and Suschitzky (1997). Classroom assistants can enable teachers to plan more small-group work, and to allow for children to receive more individual support. For example, classroom assistants can support play by working in the imaginative play area, taking on such roles as shop assistant or customer. They can work with small group 'task forces' in order to help children generate solutions in problem-solving work. They can support individual children develop art techniques, such as batik or photography, and take small groups for extended movement, dance and drama work where children will benefit from having more intensive adult support. In order to develop such approaches, classroom assistants may need further training in structuring play situations and problem solving. They may need to be made more aware of the learning processes involved in creativity and to work more collaboratively with teachers in the planning process, a point highlighted by Moyles and Suschitzky (1997: 14). This in itself will enable classroom assistants to have a deeper awareness of the focus of creative goals and processes.

Meeting group and individual needs

Creative teaching requires a successful balance of managing groups and individuals. As Alexander et al. (1992) point out, groups serve a useful function as they provide opportunities for collaborative working and problem solving among children with adults. How and why groups are formed is very important; they should, as Alexander et al. suggest, 'be appropriate to the task in hand'. Dunne and Bennett (1990) and others have pointed out that where children are seated in groups but not working together, groups can often become counterproductive and fail to lead to a greater flow of creative ideas. Group working may make individuals more 'open', as the group may encourage the individual to feel a greater sense of trust and self-worth. Palmer and Pettitt (1993: 33) note that in situations where children are not necessarily engaged in a common task such as story or poetry writing, 'conversation and consultation are helpful' and, if both are encouraged, then this may sponsor the generation of creative solutions.

Teachers need to be aware that children with low self-esteem may seek group support in order to feel needed; conversely, they may hide within the group framework to avoid any challenge. A variety of groupings should be used such as ability, friendship and interest (Ofsted 1993a: 31) to enable children to understand the various purposes and functions of group work. Teachers will need to identify group working skills so that they can plan, teach and monitor them effectively. A distinction needs to be made between being *in* groups and working *as* groups. Dunne and Bennett (1990) give a very practical guide to all types of group work and the skills needed for each.

Individual work is about developing each child's creative potential. Individual conferencing should be set up in order to discuss with each child their feelings about their own learning and creative development. Conferences should not necessarily be seen as either evaluative or routine; they should, however, provide each child with some time to respond to the teacher on a personal basis. The teacher invests time and value in these discussions, thus leading each child to a feeling of self-worth. At the same time, new avenues for ideas and creative development can be explored. Conferencing has become an accepted form of approach since the inception of the Primary Language and the Patterns of Learning Records (Barrs *et al.* 1989, 1990), both of which incorporate conferences with individual children and their parents as an integral part of the process. It has proved to be a most valuable way of eliciting children's views about language and literacy (Newman 1985).

In the next section, we look at what constitutes a good learning environment to foster children's originality, and we see how teachers have used the changing educational climate to generate many creative possibilities.

The context for developing originality

An appropriate climate for originality – the classroom

Each classroom has a particular ethos or climate, resulting from three separate aspects which, when brought together, form a learning context:

- the *physical* climate – created through the organization and management of space and resources;

- the *intellectual* climate – which provides the appropriate degree of stimulation and challenge;
- the *emotional* climate – wherein the learners' needs are met.

A climate for originality can be brought about if we see teaching as a chance for teachers to be 'creators of events in which their classes and they participate' (Frost 1997: 4). Let us consider the successful elements of each briefly in turn.

The physical climate

The classroom layout

We are aiming to create the kind of provision which Blenkin and Kelly (1994: 199) see as stimulating 'the intellectual growth of children and fully develops their capacities and their potential' by extending their 'imagination and creativity of thinking and expression'. In order to develop children's originality the layout of the room will need to provide the 'sufficiently tight framework' which enables children to be 'free to be creative' (Frost 1997: 182). Children will need to be able to express themselves in a variety of ways, for example using large spaces for building models or expressing dance ideas and small spaces for making detailed drawings, listening to tapes or reflecting on ideas. Some forms of expression, such as modelling with clay, mean that there should be provision for messy areas; other expressions may be noisy, such as puppet plays or exploring loud sounds. The layout will often need to accommodate a range of activities taking place at the same time. Here teachers can fully enjoy their role as they set up the stage on to which this whole cast of performers will enact their talents in their various ways.

Resources

As Hurst (1994) points out, 'autonomy, creativity and lateral thinking' are essential in enabling children to have the ability to adapt intelligently to new circumstances. 'Through imaginative responses to challenges and dilemmas children extend their learning beyond the current situation . . . reaching forward to new ways to achieve their goals' (p. 62). Such skills are vital to prepare children for the fast pace of technological, economic and political changes. Resources therefore will need to be available not only to develop learning in each of the curriculum areas, but also to support problem solving, imaginative play, working cooperatively and aesthetic appreciation. Many resources will be interchangeable, and this plurality of use should be encouraged. In a successful learning environment children will be encouraged to use the resources in a variety of ways with no fixed boundaries. While equipment might be stored in the maths area – for example conkers and acorns for counting – they may be used for art, science or other activities. Using resources across the curriculum in unusual ways encourages the making of connections – the second tier of creative development. Children naturally fail to see boundaries, happily using a saucepan as a hat or counters as plates of chips and, instead of rushing in with 'that's not what counters are for!' the teacher welcomes such imaginative uses. Much use should be made of freely available materials, such as leaves and shells, as well as 'junk' materials. These are not only available cheaply, but the recycling and reusing of materials in itself extends children's thinking about creative usage of materials and further encourages them to think laterally.

The intellectual climate

Children will need to be challenged in order to stimulate their abilities to think of original ideas and solutions. This is why Shallcross (1981) suggests that solo brainstorming – digging deep into the mind to dredge out ideas – is so important. The classroom can present children with intellectual challenges which progressively build on individual children's cognitive learning. Tasks can be set which enable children to perform at a higher level with peer or adult support (Vygotsky 1978), but the challenges set should be within the child's capabilities (Wood and Attfield 1996 provide a very readable account of Vygotskian principles for learning in the early years). Children need to feel success and to feel that they are acquiring learning. Those with poor motivation can be greatly aided by the teacher's provision of achievable tasks which promote original responses and gradually increasing complexities in order to build up competence and confidence. The more confident the child, the more likely they are to voice original ideas. The classroom should, therefore, provide a safe environment for risk taking, problem solving and experimentation, which will all provide the necessary challenge and opportunity for originality in approach.

The emotional climate and classroom rules

A supportive climate is generally considered most useful in encouraging original responses (Shallcross 1981: 12). It can be argued that creativity does contain an element of effort which can be painful, however worthwhile!

In Maslow's hierarchy of human needs (1954), 'creativity and self-actualization' are at the top of the scale and, as such, will only be achieved if the other more basic needs have been met. A supportive environment is one in which pupils feel it is safe to take risks, to experiment without too frequent a fear of failure and within which effort is rewarded. Risk is an important element in creativity: 'to make art at all you have to be free to make bad art. What you need to get out of the way is your fear of that which stops you doing anything' (de Bono 1996). Any child who experiences setbacks or failures needs to be able to experience success very soon after to prevent damage to self-esteem. The teacher has the responsibility to ensure that opportunities for success can quickly be achieved. 'If you are tense you can't be creative; the more relaxed you are the more doors open' (Peiffer 1996).

'Setting the stage'

In creating the climate teachers are setting the stage. The more teachers use their imaginations when organizing the room and resources, the more they use original ideas themselves, the more likely they are to create the sort of environment where children will feel equally free to go beyond the conventional. Classrooms followed a fairly rigid pattern until the analogy of the 'workshop' classroom came about. This is undoubtedly a freer structure, yet there is still more scope for organizing in original ways. Classrooms can be wild and wacky places. Learning can be fun!

Use the direct analogy method to think what else your classroom could be. Instead of confining any imaginative ideas to a corner of the room, think in terms of the whole room and follow a theme. Doing a project on animals? Then make your room a zoo. The doorway provides the entrance, a ticket desk is just inside the door, the room is divided into cages – the 'bear pen' is where the maths things are, the 'lions' den' your reading area, the 'giraffe enclosure' your science bay and so on. Simple cheap dividers can be made by fixing lengths of strong string across the room (above head height) and then pegging on large sheets of material in a washing line effect which curtains off sections of the room. If you can get plain fabric (old sheets) these can be dyed, painted, printed or crayoned – tiger stripes, leopard spots, zebra markings, footprints, pawprints or feather patterns. The scope is endless. Large scale trees can be made with rolled up newspaper and card; large scale models can be made around a base of chicken wire. Your room can be transformed quickly and cheaply.

The whole room then becomes a resource for learning. The division of the room requires skills from maths, design and technology to be brought into play. Artistic skills are brought to bear with the decoration of each section and with creating the overall 'picture' which the room presents. Reading and writing skills will naturally be an integral part of the preparation. Using the room this way gets round the often heard moan about 'no space for an imaginative play area'. Direct analogy allows you to think of the classroom space as just that: a space to be designed. How else could it be organized if it were another group of people working? An office, a factory, a shop? Is it an indoor space or an outdoor one? On the ground? In the air? It could be a garden, part of the Great Barrier Reef, an art gallery or in outer space. Enliven a music theme by turning your room into an orchestra: sections of the room become woodwind, brass, percussion, strings. The teacher becomes the conductor, organizing, leading and developing each section of the orchestra and individual soloists. What an ideal basis for looking at collaborative working. Doing a project on Morocco? Then turn the room into a souk, creating tiny enclosures for an indoor market.

Design possibilities are immediately opened up allowing for a free flow of original and imaginative ideas to be set in motion. Children will need skills from all the curriculum areas to design such 'classroom sets', and they will be able to work in small 'task force' groups to solve any potential design or organization/management problems. Dividers themselves give lots of scope for originality. Lines provide the basis for a variety of hangings. Large pieces of material, such as curtains, cloths or old dresses are easily obtained from jumble sales or car boot sales. Lengths of material can be cut from them and then woven or plaited before hanging in sections of colours, shades, textures and patterns. Paper designs can be used in a similar way. Large scale mobiles using a variety of materials (for example, foil, wood, corks, bottle tops, leaves or pasta) can be suspended on the 'washing lines', fitting in the design according to the current theme. Material can also be hung across lines to provide covering for areas or 'roofs'. Organization itself, thus, becomes a creative act giving teachers the chance to express their originality.

An appropriate climate for creativity – the wider context

Fortunately, creative teachers seem to flourish whatever the educational climate, perhaps because they can usually see original ways of handling challenge. 'Teaching is a most creative profession' notes Fryer (1996: 72), although her study showed that many teachers were unaware of having creative skills. Large numbers of teachers have grasped the wide number of changes brought about by the Education Reform Act (1988) and subsequent amendments with enthusiasm, creativity and energy. This is shown in the way teachers have found new ways forward with parents, with the community, with school organization and training. Not only do the following examples show how creative and original teachers can be, but the examples also show how new ways of working open up increased possibilities for creative classroom work.

Parents and community partnerships

Many teachers have found that the legislation which encourages parents to be seen as 'clients' allows them to adopt new approaches. As the old models have been removed so these teachers have set in place innovative and creative models of partnership (Bastiani 1989; Wolfendale 1992). Working with parents gives scope for setting up new organizations, such as home–school maths partnerships, school libraries, setting up parents' rooms or running literacy classes for parents – even having parents learning alongside children. Involving parents may also mean that their particular creative skills, for example as actors, artists, musicians or storytellers can be utilized to spark creative activities. Parents can add a different dimension to class project work by talking about their lives and experiences from their own unique standpoint. This is particularly valuable if they represent an ethnic minority culture.

Redlands Primary School, an urban school with a multi-ethnic intake, is typical of many schools which has decided to invest energy and commitment in a long term project involving parents fully as partners in all aspects of school life. This scheme was innovative, causing staff to look for ways of creating new and original patterns of involvement. It meant that teachers had to rethink their roles and had to 'place greater trust in the children's role as active learners'. Parents became a sounding board for new ideas, and with so many new voices to make suggestions many creative ideas were generated. 'Give parents the opportunity and the encouragement and they will respond enthusiastically' (Edwards and Redfern 1988: 163).

Teachers have also responded enthusiastically to the challenge of working more closely with industry and the local community. The cross-curricular theme of 'education for economic and industrial understanding' has been used to provide a new dimension through which to explore classroom projects. Depth has been given to projects, such as 'People who help us' by a study of roles and conditions of work. Using drama and imaginative play children have been given deeper understanding of the economic and social reality of, for example, the local newsagent, visiting the place of work and then acting out the way the newspaper sales are organized.

Many schools have adopted more formal links with industry. For example, local cooperative societies have arranged for primary children to take on roles within their shops, serving on cash tills, filling shelves, deciding on goods to be sold and looking at the way that money is used to buy goods, pay for staff and how much profit or loss is made. Such ventures are almost large scale imaginative play situations, giving children the experience of being in adult roles in a real life situation. *The Primary Enterprise Pack* (Ross *et al.* 1990) shows ways in which collaborative approaches can be taken with local firms. Hollickwood Primary School, for example, ran a similar project involving a local corner shop. The class shop benefited from having a working cash till loaned to them for imaginative play, and subsequent role play was imbued by a growing understanding of business needs (Ross *et al.* 1990: 6–7). Loirston Primary School involved a Year 4 class in links with an oil rig and garage. Computer-controlled Lego models were used in order to help children understand the way the garage operated. Children were set tasks which required imaginative responses, such as how to construct shelters from natural materials if shipwrecked. Practical problem solving about weight, mass and strength of materials needed in the oil rig were tested using the class water tray (pp. 25–7). These various partnership projects show how children can gain an insight into industry and community schemes which enhance their social perceptions, increase their awareness of social issues and provide a wider view of the world beyond the classroom. Such experiences enable children to make direct analogies across areas which encourage original approaches. Teachers find that sharing ideas with non-teaching adults is a stimulating and rewarding experience. There are many examples of creative classroom work which have been inspired as a result of visits and shared work experiences. Children and teachers have both found that the quality of learning has been enhanced by the chance to participate in the educational opportunities provided by outside bodies such as the National Trust (benefits mentioned in Chapter 6). These new links have been a source of creative inspiration.

Changing forms of organization

In other instances head teachers are often inspirational. Criteria for inspection clearly indicate the importance inspectors attach to the head's role (Ofsted 1995). Where head teachers are themselves innovative in approaching change they are likely to support a more open-ended approach and to adopt a creative style of management which encourages their staff to be creative too. The head teacher of Coombes County Infant and Nursery School, Susan Humphries, has been such an inspirational leader. Since 1971 the school has worked each year under her guidance in order to develop each area of the school grounds 'into an area of beauty in its own right and a rich resource for learning and development' (Woods 1995: 46). The school staff decided to rethink their organization and management so that they could use their grounds for teaching throughout the day. They wanted to create a system whereby teaching took place indoors and outdoors at all times, so that the environment was fully used as a teaching resource. This also meant having to explore creatively the way staff are deployed. Because of the head's originality of thinking and leadership, teachers and children have worked together to create an environment which enriches the curriculum and links learning to the natural world. As a result, the school has enthusiastic and motivated staff and draws on substantial parental support and community involvement.

The climate of change in education has also encouraged some creative suggestions about new forms of organization, such as the 'continental day' suggested by Blatchford (1989: 117), or the reorganization of patterns of day care suggested by Moss and Penn in their call for a 'shift of attitudes' (1996: 165). If the parameters of current organization are removed, exciting prospects for reorganization come into view. Use the direct analogy approach to summon up ways of organizing the day and the organization of the school as, for example, a department store, a library or a studio. There may well be more interesting and more productive forms to be found.

The changing context of training

Changes to teacher training have also brought additional challenges: much of the training is now focused in schools. Models of teacher training are either school-based or school-centred; many teachers have a training role. In addition the format for training has changed and is now based on competences (DfE 1993). Many teachers have seen creative openings to:

- train for a different role (as mentors they will train adults and be involved with inservice work with adults);
- extend their skills (the mentor role will give greater experience of interpersonal and communication skills);
- disseminate their experience to a wider audience (there will be opportunities to give talks to colleges, groups of parents and teachers);
- increase opportunities for further professional development, qualifications and promotion (reading, attendance on courses and further qualifications, such as masters degrees, mean increased possibilities for promotion).

In Enfield mentors have been used with primary pupils in a pilot scheme in order to raise self-esteem and boost pupil achievement: an imaginative and innovative approach which opens up more possibilities for teachers and pupils alike.

These are just a few examples. Many more original ideas for organization and management await implementation. If creativity is about pushing forward the boundaries then these examples prove that creativity is alive and well and that teachers are using every opportunity to find ways of developing originality by looking beyond the obvious.

Key considerations for assessment

Use of the following checklist will help to ensure that children are developing originality through positive approaches to change.

The child

- Does the child respond to change with enthusiasm?
- Does the child welcome new ideas and situations?
- To what extent does the child persevere when faced with a challenge?
- Does the child apply a wide range of skills and techniques, for example in art work?
- Are these skills and techniques often used in unusual ways?
- Does the child enjoy working with others in both small and large groups?
- Does the child demonstrate a need to work through their ideas alone?
- Does the child often copy ideas, or are his/her ideas copied by others?

The teacher

- Are opportunities for change seen positively?
- Is the curriculum developed to encourage adaptability, challenge and a variety of interpretation?
- Is specialist support given to children who show exceptional ability, for example musical instrument tuition or writing poetry with visiting poets?
- Are children encouraged to transfer skills, knowledge and understanding from one curriculum area to another?

The context

- Does the school/local area offer support to enhance particular skills out of school hours, for example dance classes, photography clubs and football training?
- Are there inservice opportunities for teachers and other adults to develop their own skills, knowledge and understanding in more specialist fields?
- Is there a supportive climate within the school which encourages an enthusiastic and creative approach to change?

Strategies for change

Stress – coping with change

Stress can be reduced and your needs expressed by giving yourself opportunities to:

- brainstorm all the things about the job which worry you;
- list the problems;
- ask for an inservice session to discuss your concerns with the rest of the staff (you are bound to find others who feel the same);
- look together at common problems and sort into school/classroom ones;
- rate the problems and agree on a starting point;
- set out a timescale, roles, action points and review procedure and tackle the first problem;
- tackle other problems in the same way;
- make yourself think positively about negatives;
- concentrate on your strengths and note them down;
- concentrate on the children and share their enjoyment wherever it occurs;
- decide to make teaching enjoyable and to look for ways in which you can make changes and use your ideas more – they can be found;
- use the creative arts more – they have a therapeutic role – more singing and dancing and less work cards!

Reflective journals

Reflective journals are diaries in which teachers can record any significant classroom challenges or successes. They provide an opportunity for feelings, worries and ideas to be jotted down so that they may form the basis of a discussion with colleagues at inservice sessions. Sharing feelings and realizing that others feel the same way is a great source of strength. Strategies for change can be developed as a result of reflection and discussion. Reflective journals provide:

- a means of evaluating change and development;
- space for both professional and personal commentary;
- a way of increasing self-awareness and positive self-worth;

- space for reflection;
- a basis for professional dialogue.

Key elements needed to teach creatively

Teachers will need to:

- create a physical, mental and emotional climate which supports creativity;
- provide a balanced programme which meets group and individual needs;
- provide for play and learning through action and interaction;
- plan effective programmes of work across the curriculum;
- provide and manage resources effectively;
- develop creative thinking skills;
- develop sensitivity;
- be aware of children's development;
- be open and reflective in approach;
- be able to value each child's contribution;
- be willing to see potential in themselves and in each child and to seek ways of releasing it;
- encourage the creative arts and all forms of creative expression;
- enjoy challenges;
- respond to teaching in a personal way, maintaining a sense of self-worth;
- draw on multicultural resources.

Summary

This chapter has examined the nature of originality in children and considered different levels of children's originality of creative response. It has also looked at the nature of originality in teaching and learning and shown how this is not dependent upon the teacher's or child's artistic ability. It is more a question of teachers being positive in outlook, seeing potential within children, being open to change and being able to overcome challenges and constraints. Problem solving has been shown to be a useful creative strategy. The context has been discussed in some length, firstly by considering the elements which enable a successful classroom environment to be set up and, secondly, by looking at the way teachers have used educational change to provide new avenues for creative teaching and learning. Finally, creative teaching in essence provides all children with opportunities for self-expression, and leads them to make imaginative and original connections which are the basis for new ideas. There is no need for an elite system requiring specially gifted teachers to teach specially gifted children: we can all do it!

In the final chapter, we will look at the inspiration provided by nature in enhancing everyone's creativity.

6

'Life, the universe, and 3C's sunflowers'

Creativity and nature

Cameo 1

Anna's class of 9-year-olds are hard at work outside in the school garden. The ground has been levelled, dug over and the bare earth divided into small squares, either with string or low strips of wood. Anna is helping a group of children to firm down the soil in one of these squares after they have planted some carrot seeds – the marks of the children's footprints can clearly be seen in neat rows. Five children are at the back of the area near to the hen house, the compost heap and the tool shed, working with full-sized rakes to clear the ground ready for sowing. Some children dig, again with full-sized spades; others are trowelling, hoeing, watering, collecting up stones or marking out their patches with small pieces of white paper stuck on to sticks and pushed into the soil. It is April and not yet very warm; a shower is imminent. The children's concentration is total. No matter what the weather the chickens have to be fed and the plot tended. April is an important month in the garden.

Cameo 2

Class 3C (8-year-olds) have been looking at 'Growth' as their termly theme. One corner of their classroom has a large model oak tree stretching its branches toward the ceiling and curving along the walls. It is large enough to have a child-sized opening and has room for a child to sit inside. Holes elsewhere in the branches house 'nests' for animals and birds. In another corner small pots of petunias are in full flower. A

clematis in a larger pot winds its way upwards, its purple flowers entwining with the summer jasmine in the pot nearby
whose scent fills the room. On the window ledges are various
cuttings and seedlings growing. A guinea pig nestles in its cage
next to the fish tank in a bay near the door. However, pride of
place must go to the sunflowers, whose tall stems and large
yellow heads form an unforgettable sight. They are in pots
near the window so that the light catches them. The sunflowers have provided an impetus for learning. Hanging from the
ceiling are lines of 'sunflower' petals on the back of which
there is a child's story about growing things. Along a wall there
is a series of photographs of the children with the plants at
various stages of growth forming a time line. Displays about
their mathematical and scientific investigations into the development of these sunflowers cover other parts of the walls.
Drawings and models of seed-eating birds are mounted nearby.
The book corner is full of books on growth including several
made by the children in the shape of sunflowers.

Cameo 3

It is a very windy day but not cold. Jim's Year 2 class seems a
bit excitable and slow to settle this morning, so he has taken
them outside. He has told the class to bring their sketch pads
and notebooks and to record their feelings about the weather.
Some children have brought out chairs and are sitting drawing
the scudding clouds overhead. Susie has brought out a paint-
box and is trying to mix up the colour of the school playground so she can complete her picture of the windy scene.
Mark and Sally find that it is hard to hold down the pages of
their notebooks and Simon loses his drawing in a sudden gust
of wind. Someone has noted that the wind makes a whistling
noise as it rounds the corner of the caretaker's house, and a
group have started up an impromptu chorus, imitating the
sounds. A few children are running around, rushing, swaying
and bending in the rhythm of the wind.

Introduction

In each of these cameos the children are in direct contact with the
natural world or, as in Cameo 2, a representation of it. They are
learning both in and about the environment in which they live.
This stimulates further curiosity and investigation. Creativity is
related to the act of creation, both in its widest sense (the devel-

opment of the universe) and in its smallest spark of life (the growth of a seed). This chapter will examine the benefits for children and teachers of working in a more holistic way, using nature to inspire creative learning. We will consider ways in which we can develop both the classroom and the wider school as a creative learning environment.

Nature, creativity and the child

The benefits of gardening

Gardening has obvious benefits to physical development, which in turn affects creative development. In Cameo 1 the children have plenty of space to move and to exercise their bodies with large scale movements such as digging, raking, running and bending. A well exercised body aids cognitive functioning (Connell 1989) and information processing (Bruner 1972), which is a physical process. Since children spend a lot of time sitting watching television and using computers, it is important for schools to find ways of increasing the opportunities for vigorous exercise to combat these sedentary trends (Robson and Smedley 1996). This does not mean just the old idea of 'playtime' where children were allowed to 'let off steam'. Studies such as Blatchford's (1989) have shown this approach to be a wasted learning resource. Structured opportunities for physical exertion, such as that provided by gardening (Figure 6.1), give children a natural way to develop their physical skills in a creative context. The physical release of energy enables the mind to reflect more easily and behave more creatively.

Gardening provides opportunities to create new plant life and thus to stimulate children's spiritual and emotional development. Gardening can bring children close to the meaning of spirituality – 'one is nearer God's heart in a garden than anywhere else on earth' (Dorothy Gurney) – and this makes it an essential element in developing creative children. A piece of open ground provides the blank canvas for children to try out their ideas. No one can really foretell the outcome, since growth is dependent upon so many factors: this gives gardening an element of mystery, surprise and wonder. Children have a chance to create something totally new since the patterns of growth will all be unique. Gardening can be successfully carried out within the classroom, as

Cameo 2 shows. Gardens can almost be works of art in themselves, linking the sensory with the spiritual and emotional. Opportunities to visit gardens open to the public provide a source of inspiration for curriculum work.

In gardening, mind and body are involved in creating a holistic combination 'of the pupils, of the learning and of the curriculum' (Woods 1995: 2). Working in this way gives children an extra freedom of expression which is conducive to creative development. In Cameo 1, their gardening gave children the freedom to

Figure 6.1 Children experience the cycle of growth at first hand through gardening

talk without any worries about making too much noise or disturbing others. Gardening is also a social experience in which children have a chance to create something collaboratively and to share their creative experiences.

In all three cameos the children have chances to become engaged in social groups and to express their ideas about the tasks in hand. Physical, emotional and cognitive development are closely linked as the children express their feelings, respond to the experiences, discuss their ideas and gradually develop an understanding of how things grow or how the weather behaves. Wheatley (1992) was inspired by this type of environmental education. Working outside provides a sensory environment where children are exposed to changes in light, temperature and elements of the weather and to a range of auditory and visual images. The visual perspective is wider, further distances are involved and thus the child's focus is broadened.

Working outside provides an emotional climate which is different from indoors. Outside, children are exposed to the wider world and become a part of that environment. Saying that they are more 'at one with nature' sums up these qualities. Creative thought often flourishes with access to such wider perspectives. These children are learning about how to fertilize the soil, the species of birds which eat sunflower seeds and the sound made by the wind. They are engaged in learning, using all their senses in a holistic way (Hazareesingh 1991).

Creation – a source of wonder and inspiration

The cycle of life in all its profundity is demonstrated in a small way through the act of planting seeds and watching them grow, stimulating the imagination in the same way that Egan (1992) suggests that the cycle of tree growth does. The gardening class will be able to harvest their vegetables and to rear their chicks to adulthood. 3C have been able to see how a sunflower seed has produced a huge plant, a dramatically colourful flower and seeds ready to plant again. They have planted bulbs and taken cuttings, learning of other ways of starting new plants. They have looked at the interrelatedness of plant and animal life with the 'nests' in the oak tree and seed-eating birds. Jim's class have been made very aware of the effects of the weather both on the environment and on their own feelings. Jim has encouraged his class to respond directly to nature by asking them to note how they feel. In their sketches and notes the children are directly recording their sensory experiences in all their breadth and depth. In a small way, all of these children are able to experience just how tiny a part of the whole universe they are and yet to understand just how important each tiny part is within the whole.

The sensory nature of the responses felt when in direct contact with the natural world provide inspiration for creative work. It enables children to build upon their natural curiosity and natural tendency to 'touch and hold things to manipulate them and include them in their play' (Gentle 1985: 53). The part played by 'nature' as an inspirational force is a huge one. Consider the relationship between painters and the landscape, sculptors and the human form, poets and flowers – the patterns, shapes, colours, sizes and textures of leaves, for example, or the variety of animal movements. Each provides such a range that they are an ever present source of inspiration for creative people. Artists try to capture the complex facets of the human and natural environment, using not only their technical skills but also their ability to relate to and interpret these complexities. Fortunately the sources of this inspiration are all around us and readily available for classroom use. 3C's sunflowers are a stimulus for maths and scientific investigation and a source for calculation, measurement and prediction. Even in the most constrained of classroom conditions it is possible to grow sunflowers.

The importance of first-hand experience

Working with nature allows children to have a huge variety of first-hand experiences enabling them to build up rich sensory images of the world and to focus intently. The use of first-hand experience is essential to all areas of the curriculum but especially to art (Gentle 1985). Whether children respond in a primarily visual, tactile, auditory or spatial way will depend on the child. What is certain is that the memory of the experience can be sharply recalled, not just as shape, colour or texture, but in the particulars of smell and the associations of noises and other aspects of that time. There is 'a totality of recall involving associations and memories which can never be quite the same when derived from a second-hand experience such as from television or pictures in books' (Gentle 1985: 8). The children in 3C are able to respond to the sunflowers and to be inspired by them in the same way as was Van Gogh and many other artists.

3C's experience of sunflowers is also a shared one; the social setting of the classroom provides security, support and a chance to share feelings of awe and wonder. Such feelings give the memory its intensity, making it likely that the experience will be retained in the long term memory. Since learning can be seen as a three-stage process where the learner first engages, then stores and processes information in the short term memory before finally retaining it in the long term memory (Kyriacou 1991), the importance of employing techniques which lead to information being retained and concepts formed and re-formed, cannot be overemphasized.

Using natural resources

Creativity is not always dependent upon sophisticated resources; indeed, quite the opposite can be true. As children explore materials without outcomes, they will use their imaginations (Lancaster 1987). The wind provided a simple and free resource for Jim's class to explore sound, movement and natural forces. All the plants grown in 3C and in Anna's garden cost little more than packets of seeds; the cuttings were freely and readily available. Yet they provided simple but stimulating opportunities for understanding the growth of living things. Earth, water, air, the weather, light and sound are ever present, all around us and freely available. Responding to these elements provides children with almost the only resources they will need to begin to 'create' for themselves from their own images.

Natural materials such as wood, clay, sand and water lend themselves to free exploration and to the development of children's imaginative interpretation. They have properties which 'are highly conducive to creative play' (Moyles 1989: 79). The children in the first two cameos have ample experience of handling the soil, using it to create new plant growth. Soil is one of the most basic and primary elements of the natural and man-made environment. Writing as long ago as 1970, Yardley describes how children go through a process of absorbing before mastering the materials. They are then able to 'handle materials in a way which is truly creative' (p. 36). She sees the educative value as being inherent in the materials themselves. They have qualities which, in Gentle's words (1985: 55), 'shape and modify a child's ideas' in a two-way process as the child moulds the material. Children in the cameos are responding to nature and being governed by its forces, the wind, the soil, the seasons. Yet they are at the same time shaping it, digging the ground and altering its layout, making new plants grow and learning to protect themselves against the weather. This has particular implications for the teacher.

Nature, creativity and the teacher

In the classroom

3C's teacher has clearly seen the potential of surrounding her children with growing things. Her small classroom (with the usual constraints of fixed cupboards, radiators and high window ledges) has almost become an extension of the outside. She has been flexible with the classroom layout: she has used the full height of the room, building the tree right up to the ceiling and hanging the sunflower petal stories as high banners. Corners have been used and the furniture arranged so that children can work in bays and small areas, such as inside the tree. The walls and surface areas are covered with children's written work, models and art work, yet everything is organized so that in the wealth of display everybody knows just where everything is.

The children in 3C have been encouraged to take care of the classroom by a rigorous rota system. Everyone has a turn at doing all the jobs, watering the plants, feeding and cleaning out the guinea pigs and the fish, tidying up the odd corners (where pencils lurk and bits of collage get lodged). The children have all been taught how to mount their work and use the displays as an extension of the creative process. In making decisions about how items should be displayed, the children are developing highly critical eyes. Teachers can find themselves with no more work than usual, and may even find they have less, if they organize the children in managing the room (Moyles 1992).

3C's teacher has also recognized the important role that animals can play in motivating children's learning and in helping them to express their feelings. Children are fascinated by plant and animal growth. Visits to nearby parks can enrich creative experience. A teacher comments on the science task she set children:

> The task was to create a home for an animal. The homes they made were quite original and the children approached

the task with their usual lack of inhibition. Some of the nests were quite beautiful, being almost living sculptures, made from grass, feathers, rhododendron petals and so on. Some children made wigwams with stick frameworks and grass coverings. One class even made molehills. They found crannies in tree trunks. None of them seemed to expect an animal to actually come and live there. The act of creation was enough in itself.

If it is not possible to have animals in the classroom it may be possible to adopt animals in local zoos, parks or farms. Organizations such as the RSPCA and the Cats' Protection League encourage sponsorship, as they have to care for many unwanted animals. This can be an excellent way of promoting responsibility and demonstrating what is involved in looking after animals. In discussing the animals' needs children can be helped to express their own needs and worries in a non-threatening way. For example, the fear of being abandoned may be a very real one for some children: in considering the role of these caring groups for abandoned animals they may be helped towards a greater understanding of their own feelings.

Animals within school have a value in promoting caring, sharing, empathy and love, and as such should be welcomed. They provide opportunities for imaginative writing, motivation and inspiration for close observational drawings. The links between animals and their natural habitats provide opportunities for outdoor study, albeit most frequently a study of local insects and mini-beasts.

Using the outside for classroom work

Teachers need to be able to see the potential of using the outside areas as a creative curriculum learning resource (Adams 1990). Once we begin to see this potential it seems odd that we expect children to learn indoors and to 'play' outside in sterile spaces. Gardening as a subject has particular potential. It was once on the curriculum and still is in some countries. Gardening may not be compulsory but it provides a framework within which all the subjects of the compulsory curriculum can be met. In setting up gardening, schools can gain inspiration from *Learning Through Landscapes* (Adams 1990), which promotes the development of school grounds through research, projects and publications. There are also many examples across the country of schools which have transformed their grounds in a variety of imaginative ways providing opportunities for creativity.

Teachers may need to look closely at the way in which the timetable is organized. Instead of dividing the day into indoor classroom and outside playground time, it needs to be determined holistically. Research into the balance of time allocated to various activities in the timetable has proved fruitful (Alexander 1982; Tizard *et al.* 1988; Blatchford 1989). Their studies show that playtime is among the 'wasted' time of the school day – Alexander puts this as high as 60 per cent. In most schools the clear distinction between classroom and playground is also marked by activities associated with each, usually called 'work' and 'play'. Jim and Anna have made no such distinctions. For them the playground is a part of the classroom. The learning which takes place outside deepens and extends the learning within the classroom. They are part of a growing band of teachers who have been able to look at alternatives to fixed period playtimes – giving children choice, cutting out afternoon play, shortening the lunch break and moving towards the 'continental' day – all very readably discussed in Blatchford (1989: 106). He notes that, as with most new ideas, thinking creatively about their playground times proved to be challenging for teachers, but it seems to me to be fundamental for primary schools. Nursery schools and classes have always been run or managed on the basis that indoors and out were essential for learning.

The playground gives much-needed space for the development of gross motor skills and thus supports learning in dance, PE and drama. Noisier activities, such as using musical instruments, large scale constructive play and experiments with sound, can be more freely explored without the worry of disturbing others. The quality of work in drama and dance is likely to be enhanced by working in the open air because the children's imagination is extended through the amount of space available (Bilton 1994) and because of the difference in acoustics. This helps voice projection because children have to learn to transmit their voices over a wider area and to compete with a certain amount of external noise.

Working outdoors gives emotional benefits which are often overlooked. Stacey and Andre both show an emotional response in their drawings of their school (Figure 6.2).

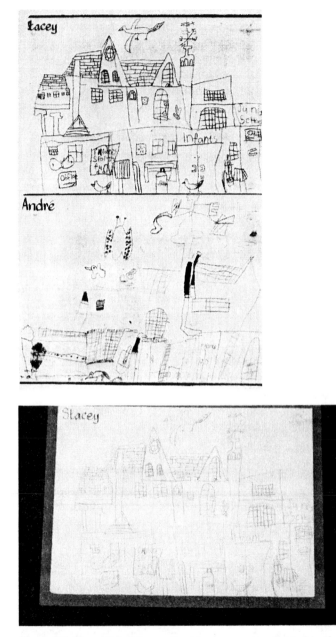

Figure 6.2 The children's emotional response is reflected in their drawings

As teachers we should make sure that children have every opportunity for outdoor activity by keeping a supply of warm clothing in school and ensuring that all children are adequately dressed for outdoor activities. Parents will need to know that wellington boots may often be needed!

The effects of weather on mood and motivation

Jim and Anna are working *with* nature rather than trying to carry on indoors in spite of the high winds which might have made the children loathe to sit at their desks. Teachers have always been very aware of the effect of the weather on children's behaviour – such comments as 'They are so morose on wet days', 'They are so excitable with the snow, I just had to let them paint' are part of the folklore of teaching. Teachers take advantage of exceptionally sunny days, of snow, high winds and storms as motivation for the curriculum in art, music, writing and drama. In such conditions children are emotionally charged, making them more enthusiastic, motivated, excited and active. Hence Jim and Anna's move from the more sedentary, routine tasks to the more active, creative ones.

Being creative is about being responsive to mood and atmosphere, searching for meaning in experience (Rowe and Newton 1994) – any analysis of the work of artists, writers, musicians and inventors reveals this clearly. They have expressed these moods, and the weather has been an influence on their urge to create or represent. Put simply, it may be very difficult for some people to respond at all on dull, cold, 'grey' days. Others may find hot, humid days inhibit all desire to respond. This is because changes in temperature and atmospheric conditions alter the body's physical and mental make-up. These are often so slight or so rooted in the subconscious that we fail to notice them but our responses are affected. Levels of light have been shown to have a profound effect on some people, as the discovery of SAD (Seasonal Affective Disorder) suggests. We now accept that this causes depression in adults and perhaps in children. Like adults, they will certainly be affected by long periods of low light which tends to depress, whereas bright light tends to enthuse and inspire.

Creative artists amply demonstrate an awareness of light, for example Impressionist painters like Monet, who became almost obsessed with the light on the water lilies in his garden; it is there,

---

also, in Yeats's poem[1] 'The blue the dim and the dark cloths/Of night and light and the half-light', Grieg's 'Morning' (from the *Peer Gynt Suite*) and Vivaldi's 'Spring' (from *The Four Seasons*), connecting the light to the time of day or the seasons. Weather, time and season all have profound inspirational effects upon creativity. All nature's elements have influenced works in the fields of art, music, drama, poetry and literature.

Weather often has quite dramatic effects on motivation: without the 'right' conditions it may be impossible to respond. The artist/creator is instinctively aware of this and waits for the right atmosphere to occur before seizing the moment. It is obviously impossible for us as teachers to cater for individual responses in this way, but we can be more aware of the overall effects of weather and its changes (some suggestions for using the weather more are discussed in the Strategies for change section). If, like Jim and Anna, we are prepared to move the curriculum outside on a regular basis, it is likely that we will meet most of the children's needs to respond more physically and emotionally to their environment. Responding in this way can prevent children from becoming restless or disruptive. It can also increase motivation, pro-social behaviour and soothe aggressive tendencies.

Teachers in the UK are often unused to taking their children outside in inclement or adverse weather conditions. This is in marked contrast to Norway, for example, where children are taught outdoors, often in sub-zero temperatures. The teachers there say that 'there is no such thing as bad weather, only bad clothing'. Norwegian children are used to being dressed appropriately in boots, hats, gloves and snow suits, and weather is not seen as a problem.

It need not be a problem in the UK either. Schools all have requirements for plimsolls for PE lessons. They could equally well ask for boots for outdoor lessons. School uniform requirements could easily include hats, scarves and gloves for cold weather, sun hats for hot days and waterproof coats or jackets. Discussing the appropriate requirements and designing them could form an excellent school art/design/technology project involving all staff, children and parents in thinking about new ways of using the outside areas.

Developing a whole-school management policy can simplify the organizational aspects. If the school building is seen as a site where there is a flexible use of personnel – rather than separate classrooms, each with a fixed person attached to it – then it becomes possible to draw up cover rotas for each separate area, including the outside. Historically this was considered important. The 'Open Air' Nursery School opened in Deptford by Margaret McMillan in 1914 provided a blueprint for much nursery and infant school building until the 1950s (Bradburn 1976: 50). Children's health was considered integral to their ability to learn. This has not changed to the present day, yet curricular needs often override considerations of health and physical needs.

Developing the school building, the grounds and using the local environment is considered in the next section.

Creativity in the context of nature

The school building

While the individual teacher has the freedom to organize the classroom to reflect the natural world in an exciting and inspiring way, many of the most long-lasting changes depend upon a whole-school approach. Each classroom can have a creative ethos, but the school needs to support this to develop the full range of children's potential. A school ethos demonstrates its value of creativity through:

- imaginative and colourful displays of work;
- a stimulating environment;
- supporting problem-solving and investigative approaches.

If the school environment reflects a love of the natural world it will affect the teachers and children within each classroom.

Sometimes schools with difficult buildings or poor outdoor facilities may feel the odds are against them. Schools in poor repair and needing redecoration can still be transformed if staff and governors are determined to create an exciting environment and give priority to the task. Unattractive colours or eyesores (such as pipes) can be disguised by tubs of plants; unsightly bits of wall can be covered by card, wood or trellis in order to mount displays. It is not always necessary to redecorate the building – camouflage can be effective!

Delegation of budgets to schools has meant that they are now in competition with one another to recruit and maintain pupil numbers. It is likely that schools which present attractive external images will be more favourably viewed by prospective parents. For both commercial and aesthetic reasons, therefore, it may be in everyone's interests to take a long hard look at the way in which the school appears to the wider community.

The entrance to the school is very important. It is worth thinking about the impression given by the entrance. Exterior walls can be brightened by murals. They can be fixed with trellis or wires so that climbing plants can be grown in tubs. Just think of walking through a school entrance that was surrounded by a wisteria in full bloom – the sight and scent in the spring would be unforgettable! Hooks to support hanging baskets and window boxes can be easily fitted, pots can surround the doorways. Welcome notices, direction signs and use of community languages, where appropriate, are another sign that the school is concerned with how people feel and respond to their environment as well as how they learn.

Developing the outside area

In guiding the developments outlined by Woods (1995) and Blatchford (1989), the teachers at Coombes Infant and Nursery School have been guided by the Froebelian principle that 'nature study is a means to understanding the unity of creation' (Woods 1995: 54). This led schools prior to the National Curriculum to set up nature tables and to have projects on the seasons. Seasonal patterns can still be seen in schools through religious festivals, but there are no statutory requirements to follow 'nature study'. Much of this response to seasonal patterns has therefore been forgotten or overlaid by other considerations. Not so at Coombes, where they have interpreted the statutory curriculum to develop more holistic learning patterns which respond to the seasons and to the cycle of growth, life and death.

There are huge variations in the way schools are designed and in the amount of space that surrounds the building. Some schools are well endowed with large areas which provide grassed patches, trees and flower beds. Anna's school has enough space for garden plots. Others have little more than concrete and tarmac. Most are somewhere in between. Every area has the potential for creative development, for example in display, decoration and especially in gardening and landscaping, though it may require a good deal of creative thinking to recognize it! George Spicer School has created an attractive garden and pond area by building a raised bed in the centre of the playground. The surrounding mesh fences have tubs, seats and climbing plants (a mesh fence provides the ideal climbing support for roses, ivy and clematis). Every school has the potential for container gardening, and there are a wealth of garden writers to inspire them (see Strategies for change section).

Links with commercial companies such as seed merchants can be invaluable, as can community programmes. George Spicer School took part in the 'Enfield in Bloom' scheme, along with many other local schools. Such outside projects often give the impetus to develop schools' outdoor environments. Similarly, 3C had taken part in flower-growing competitions sponsored by seed companies. Bodies such as the Royal Horticultural Society run school garden competitions. For those schools interested in achievement or the achievement ethic, such projects provide excellent motivation. The children who have been inspired to grow the tallest sunflower may well continue their creative interests through gardening.

The wider environment

Community schemes often involve improving areas of the local environment outside the school, such as bulb or tree planting, developing areas of waste ground or sponsored flower beds. These schemes provide excellent opportunities for involving children in the community and in developing their aesthetic awareness by creating pleasant spaces in their local area. They provide opportunities for children to consider the built environment in more detail and to extend their range of understanding. Primary age children usually have a deep concern for their surroundings and, if encouraged, are able to think of many imaginative ways of making areas 'green'.

Visits to local open areas will increase children's awareness and provide ideas for them to develop further in school. Seeing and appreciating a variety of environments – open land, parks, woods and housing estates, for example – develops children's understanding of land use and space. The wider the experience the more scope children will have for developing critical faculties and for using these experiences in designing, planning and prob-

Figure 6.3 Being with animals can promote attitudes of caring, empathy, warmth and responsibility

lem solving. Children have an important contribution to make in critically reviewing local parks and other such leisure facilities; they can help suggest ways to improve them as well as obviously enjoying the spacious, green environment.

If your school possesses large grounds or borders open land, consider increasing children's understanding of animal husbandry either by adopting an animal or running a mini-school farm in the way that city farms have been developed. This could be seen as a commercial enterprise in the same way and might therefore be cost-effective. City farms give children from urban areas the chance to share in the care and upbringing of animals, which will enhance children's creative approaches. Both urban and rural schools can take full advantage of the educational opportunities offered by farming (Figure 6.3).

Key considerations for assessment

The following checklist will help to ensure that nature is being used effectively to enhance creativity.

The child

- Is the child able to draw on aspects of the natural world to aid creative expression?
- Do children demonstrate an empathy with, and an understanding of, the natural world which is likely to increase their range of interpretation?
- Does the child have a natural interest in the environment, both natural and human?
- Does the child demonstrate different aspects of creativity in different environmental settings, such as the classroom, the playground and on local visits?

The teacher

- Is there sufficient freedom allowed within the curriculum to respond to changes, such as the seasons, weather and individual or collective moods?
- Are sufficient opportunities provided for children to respond to the natural environment and to focus closely on plants and animals, for example to develop multi-sensory skills?

The context

- Is there a balance of teaching in a range of contexts, for example the classroom, outside areas and visits away from the school site?
- Does the classroom reflect an appreciation of the natural world through its provision of resources and visual imagery?
- Are children being encouraged to use their creative talents to develop their local environment, whether it is their classroom, playground or community area?

Strategies for change

Skills development from first-hand experience of the natural world

- Develop close observational skills – each child must be able to 'see'.
- Encourage focus – by presenting the detail of the very small parts of the larger object, for example talk about the ears of a rabbit before building up a picture of the whole of the rabbit.

Children do this naturally – note how they'll see an ant on a flower rather than the flower you've noticed.

- Develop descriptive language alongside the observation as outlined in language circles (see Chapter 1).
- Develop awareness of variety within a narrow focus, for example the different types and variety of apple, varieties of daffodil.
- Develop attitudes of wonder, amazement and enthusiasm for such variety.
- Develop skills of discrimination between kinds of birds (for example types of feathers), shades of lilac – auditory, visual, olfactory, tactile and sapiditory discrimination can be accompanied by the appropriate descriptive language.

Using the weather to enhance learning

- Encourage children to go outside in a variety of weathers (see notes about clothing in this chapter).
- Record weather on a daily basis, noting changes throughout the day. (Many weather charts record only one aspect, such as sunny for the whole day: this is rarely the case.)
- Encourage accurate and discriminatory recording – when did the weather change? What happened? Did it change again? Use a form of chart that can note these changes.
- Use these recordings for children to note how they feel (diary and discussion work).
- Discuss these feelings in relation to work patterns, so that children are more aware of cause and effect.
- Work with children at 'conferencing' times to see if there are patterns of response which affect their work in order to propose strategies for maximizing work.
- Consider with the class how to maximize productive moods and atmospheres; discuss how to increase motivation at nonproductive times.
- Develop each individual child's sensitivity and awareness of the effect of weather/mood/atmosphere on them, thus increasing their ability to respond emotionally.

Setting up a school garden

Include a variety of different types of plants for different sensory learning purposes:

Plants that smell

- spring bulbs such as hyacinth, daffodils, crocus, tulip;
- roses, sweet peas, stocks, sweet williams, pinks, lily of the valley, lilies;
- herbs such as thyme, mint, curry plant, sage, verbena.

Shrubs and plants that attract birds

- cotoneaster, pyracantha, holly (for berries);
- honeysuckle, potted laurel, small conifers, viburnum;
- ceanothus to provide cover and nesting sites.

Plants that attract butterflies

- buddleia, ice plants (*sedum spectabile*), hyssop, lavender, limnanthes, African marigolds.

Fruit trees for blossom and fruit and to attract bees

- apple, pear, plum, cherry, peach (all these can be obtained as dwarf trees and grown in containers).

Pond area with space for marginal plants

- marginal plants – water mint, iris, kingcups, forget-me-not;
- water plants – water lily, water crowfoot;
- oxygenating weed such as Canadian pondweed.

Arches, pergolas and trellis for climbing plants

- climbers – roses, honeysuckle, jasmine, clematis, wisteria, sweet peas. (Such fixtures give height to the garden, taking the eye upwards and also give some shade.)

Area for vegetable growing

- French beans, radish, runner beans, short carrots, spring onions, spinach, beet, turnips and potatoes – these can all be grown in small spaces and containers. (Many vegetables now come in miniature form.)
- Tomatoes, peppers, beetroot, cabbage, lettuce can all be grown in pots.
- Bean sprouts, mustard and cress, leaf radish can all be grown on the window sill.

All these plants thrive in containers with regular watering and feeding.

Bird boxes for nesting

- Try a variety for robins, tits, house martins, flycatchers.
- Fix up a bird table and bird feeders. Let children find out about the size of entrance for different species. Consider a bat box to encourage bats.

Seats, trestle tables, picnic areas and shaded areas

- It is important for children to have places to work and play out of direct sunlight to minimize risks of skin cancer.

Compost area

- Use slatted wooden containers, plastic compost bins or specially designed plastic compost sacks.
- Compost heaps are essential for helping children to understand the cycles of decay and regeneration.

Shed or somewhere to store tools.

Summary

The links between creativity and the natural world as a source of inspiration have been explored. We have seen how much the external world impinges upon the inner world. Where children and teachers are in harmony with their surroundings, they become both more contented and more motivated. Children's physical and emotional development can be nurtured alongside the creative by making full use of natural resources. For teachers 'nature' provides ample, free resources which can be used to enhance learning across the curriculum. It also provides opportunities for developing creative skills, such as close observation. The outside area of a school – sharing the complex interrelatedness of nature itself – can provide a rich source for cross-curricular projects, meeting not only curriculum targets but also enhancing the quality of life for learners – and teachers. The learning context can be enhanced by landscaping grounds and making use of surrounding natural facilities. Through studying the details of natural objects like sunflowers, children begin to understand and appreciate some of the complexities and wonders of creation. This is the true meaning of creativity.

Note

1 From 'He wishes for the cloths of heaven', in W.B. Yeats (1962) *Selected Poetry*. London: Macmillan.

Conclusion

> Parmenides didn't even believe things when he saw them.
> He believed that our senses give us an incorrect picture of
> the world, a picture that does not tally with reason. As a
> philosopher, he saw it as his task to expose all forms of per-
> ceptual illusion. This unshakeable faith in human reason is
> called rationalism. A rationalist is someone who believes
> that human reason is the primary source of knowledge of
> the world.

Thus does Sophie learn about the arguments of the senses ver-
sus reason in *Sophie's World* (Gaarder 1995: 5–6), a debate that
underpins the place of subjects in our curriculum. The present climate is one that supports the rationalist view; it mistrusts the
world of the senses. This book has been about looking seriously
at the world of the senses and examining the way sensory experiences enrich the world of reason. This holistic view emphasizes
that a full picture of the world is only gained through the interplay of mind and senses. Creativity inhabits the world of the
senses. If we do not give full weight to creativity, we are only seeing half the picture and we are, therefore, only half-educating
children.

There are three reasons why we as teachers should be promoting creativity in schools:

1 Our education system needs to regain the 'balance' required by
   the National Curriculum. We need to develop all-round

human beings. We need to emphasize creative subjects and creative ways of working. Schools are in danger of delivering a diet of learning which is removed from human experience and response. Bodies of knowledge must be supported by an understanding of the way in which experience shapes our culture.

2   In a period of anxiety about economic achievement and concern over achieving a competitive place in world markets it is important to look at the way in which creative thought can enrich economic potential. If education is about educating people for the workplace, then creative skills and creative thinkers are much needed.

3   Creativity is required for social reasons. Creativity has been shown to be a positive energy force, a means of unleashing more-productive elements of personality and of providing positive attitudes. Creativity can provide an alternative lifestyle, a means of coping with an increasingly fraught social climate, with all the stresses of modern life. In times of high unemployment, people need to know how to lead fulfilled lives when they are not working.

Worries still remain over underachievement – a personal and social tragedy. National testing appears to reveal that too many children are failing to reach their potential. Creative avenues must be explored to give all children the chance to achieve some level of success and to open up greater possibilities for broader interpretations of learning.

It is our duty, as responsible teachers, to promote creativity as a right for every child.

References

Abbs, P. (1989) *The Symbolic Order; A Contemporary Reader in the Arts Debate*. London: Falmer Press.

Ackers, J. (1994) Why involve me? – encouraging children and their parents to participate in the assessment process, in L. Abbott and R. Rodger (eds) *Quality Education in the Early Years*. Buckingham: Open University Press.

Adams, E. (1990) *Learning Through Landscapes: A Report on the Use, Design, Management and Development of School Grounds*. Winchester: Learning Through Landscapes Trust.

Alexander, R. (1982) *Policy and Practice in Primary Education*. London: Routledge.

Alexander, R., Rose, J. and Woodhead, C. (1992) *Curriculum Organisation and Classroom Practice – a Discussion Paper*. London: DES.

Anghileri, J. (1995) *Children's Mathematical Thinking in the Primary Years*. London: Cassell.

Athey, C. (1990) *Extending Thought in Young Children*. London: Paul Chapman.

Barnes, R. (1987) *Teaching Art to Young Children*. London: Allen and Unwin.

Barrow, R. (1990) *Understanding Skills: Thinking, Feeling and Caring*. London, Ontario: Althouse Press.

Barrs, M., Ellis, S., Hester, H. and Thomas, A. (1989) *Primary Language Record*. London: ILEA/CLPE.

Barrs, M., Ellis, S., Hester, H. and Thomas, A. (1990) *Patterns of Learning*. London: ILEA/CLPE.

Bartholomew, L. and Bruce, T. (1993) *Getting to Know You*. London: Hodder and Stoughton.

Bash, L., Coulby, D. and Jones, C. (1985) *Urban Schooling*. London: Holt, Rinehart and Winston.

Bastiani, J. (1989) *Working with Parents: A Whole School Approach*. Windsor: NFER Nelson.

Bastiani, J. and Wolfendale, S. (eds) (1996) *Home–School Work in Britain*. London: David Fulton.

Beetlestone, F. (1985) 'A study of the Cypriot Community in Haringey with special reference to the early years of schooling'. Unpublished thesis, University of London, Institute of Education.

Beetlestone, F. (1993) *Bright Ideas – History Projects*. Leamington Spa: Scholastic.

Beetlestone, F. (1995a) Unpublished research material on science packs.

Beetlestone, F. (1995b) Unpublished research material on early years classrooms.

Bilton, H. (1994) The nursery class garden – designing and building an outdoor environment for young children, *Early Years*, 14(2): 34–7.

Bilton, T., Bonnett, K., Jones, P., Stanworth, M., Sheard, K. and Webster, A. (1981) *Introducing Sociology*. Basingstoke: Macmillan.

Blatchford, P. (1989) *Playtime in the Primary School*. Windsor: NFER/Nelson.

Blenkin, G.M. and Kelly, A.V. (eds) (1994) *The National Curriculum and Early Learning: An Evaluation*. London: Paul Chapman.

Board of Education (1938) *Report of the Consultative Committee on Infant and Nursery Schools*. The Hadow Report. London: HMSO.

Bowles, S. and Gintis, H. (1976) *Schooling in Capitalist America*. London: Routledge and Kegan Paul.

Bradburn, E. (1976) *Margaret McMillan*. Redhill: Denholm House Press.

Brain, J. and Martin, M.D. (1983) *Child Care and Health* (2nd edition). London: Hulton.

Brierley, J. (1984) *Human Birthright: Giving the Young Brain a Chance*. London: BAECE.

Brierley, J. (1987) *Give Me a Child Until He is Seven*. Lewes: Falmer Press.

Browne, N. and France, N. (1986) *Untying the Apron Strings*. Buckingham: Open University Press.

Bruce, T. (1987) *Early Childhood Education*. London: Hodder and Stoughton.

Bruce, T. (1991) *Time to Play in Early Childhood Education*. London: Hodder and Stoughton.

Bruner, J. (1972) The nature and uses of immaturity, *American Psychologist*, 27: 687–708.

Bruner, J. (1975) *Towards a Theory of Instruction*. Cambridge, MA: Harvard University Press.

Bruner, J. (1990) *Acts of Meaning*. Cambridge, MA: Harvard University Press.

Burton, L. (1986) *Girls into Maths Can Go*. London: Cassell.

Calouste Gulbenkian Foundation (1982) *The Arts in Schools: Principles, Practice and Provision*. The Gulbenkian Report. London: Calouste Gulbenkian Foundation.

Campbell, R. (1995) *Reading in the Early Years Handbook*. Buckingham: Open University Press.

Campbell, R.J., Evans, L., Neill, Dr. S.R.St.J. and Packwood, A. (1993) *The Use and Management of Infant Teachers' Time: Some Policy Issues*. Warwick Papers on Education Policy No. 3. Stoke on Trent: Trentham Books.

Connell, R. (1989) The child in the teaching–learning process, in A. Williams (ed.) *Issues in Physical Education for the Primary Years*. London: The Falmer Press.

Cortazzi, M. (1995) Do we have to write about it now?, in J. Moyles (ed.) *Beginning Teaching, Beginning Learning*. Buckingham: Open University Press.

David, T., Curtis, A. and Siraj-Blatchford, I. (1993) *Effective Teaching in the Early Years*. OMEP.

de Bono, E. (1971) *The Use of Lateral Thinking*. Harmondsworth: Penguin.

de Bono, E. (1996) quoted in 'Portrait of the artist as a tortured soul' by M. Seaton, *Independent on Sunday*, 7 April 1996.

Department for Education [DFE] (1993) *The Initial Training of Primary School Teachers: New Criteria for Courses*. Circular 14/93. London: HMSO.

Department for Education (1994) *Our Children's Education – The Updated Parents' Charter*. London: HMSO.

Department for Education (1995) *Key Stages 1 and 2 of the National Curriculum*. London: HMSO.

Department for Education and Science (1967) *Children and Their Primary Schools*. The Plowden Report, vols 1 and 2. London: HMSO.

Department for Education and Science (1985a) *The Curriculum from 5–16* (2nd edition). Curriculum Matters 2. London: HMSO.

Department for Education and Science (1985b) *Education for All*. The Swann Report. London: HMSO.

Department for Education and Science (1988) *The Education Reform Act*. London: HMSO.

Department for Education and Science (1989) *Girls Learning Mathematics*. London: HMSO.

Department for Education and Science (1990) *Starting with Quality*. The Rumbold Report. London: HMSO.

Department for Education and Employment/School Curriculum and Assessment Authority (1996) *Desirable Outcomes for Children's Learning*. London: DfEE/SCAA.

Disability Discrimination Act (1995) London: HMSO.

Donaldson, M. (1978) *Children's Minds*. London: Flamingo.

Drummond, M.J. (1993) *Assessing Children's Learning*. London: David Fulton.

Dunne, E. and Bennett, H.N. (1990) *Talking and Learning in Groups*. London: Macmillan.

Edwards, A. and Knight, P. (1994) *Effective Early Years Education*. Buckingham: Open University Press.

Edwards, V. and Redfern, A. (1988) *At Home in School*. London: Routledge.

Egan, B. (1990) Design and technology in the primary classroom: equalizing opportunies, in E. Tutchell (ed.) *Dolls and Dungarees*. Buckingham: Open University Press.

Egan, K. (1988) *Teaching as Storytelling*. London: Routledge.

Egan, K. (1992) *Imagination in Teaching and Learning: Ages 8–15*. London: Routledge.

Egan, K. and Nadaner, D. (1988) *Imagination and Education*. Buckingham: Open University Press.

Epstein, D. (1993) *Changing Classroom Cultures*. Stoke on Trent: Trentham Books.

French, J. (1990) *The Education of Girls*. London: Cassell.

Frost, J. (1997) *Creativity in Primary Science*. Buckingham: Open University Press.

Fryer, M. (1996) *Creative Teaching and Learning*. London: Paul Chapman Publishing.

Gaarder, J. (1995) *Sophie's World*. London: Phoenix House.

Gammage, P. and Meighan, J. (1993) *Early Childhood Education: Taking Stock*. Ticknall: Education Now Books.

Gardner, H. (1978) *Developmental Psychology*. Boston, MA: Little, Brown.

Gardner, H. (1983) *Frames of Mind: The Theory of Multiple Intelligences*. New York: Basic Books.

Gardner, H. (1993) *Multiple Intelligences*. New York: Basic Books.

Garvey, C. (1977) *Play*. London: Fontana.

Gentle, K. (1985) *Children and Art Teaching*. Beckenham: Croom Helm.

Gipps, C., Brown, M., McCallum, B. and McAlister, S. (1995) *Intuition or Evidence?* Buckingham: Open University Press.

Glasser, W. (1992) *The Quality School*. New York: Harper Perennial.

Glasser, W. (1993) *The Quality School Teacher*. New York: Harper Perennial.

Goldstein, J.H. (1994) *Toys, Play and Child Development*. Cambridge: Cambridge University Press.

Graves, D.H. (1983) *Writing: Teachers and Children at Work*. Portsmouth, NH: Heinemann Educational.

Griffiths, A. and Hamilton, D. (1984) *Parent, Teacher, Child*. London: Methuen.

Guilford, J.P. (1957) Creative abilities in the arts, *Psychological Review*, 64: 110–18.

Gura, P. (ed.) (1992) *Exploring Learning: Young Children and Block Play*. London: Paul Chapman.

Hagness, R. (1994) *The Core Curriculum for Primary, Secondary and Adult Education in Norway*. Oslo: The Royal Ministry of Church, Education and Research.

Hall, N. and Abbott, L. (eds) (1991) *Play in the Primary Curriculum*. London: Hodder and Stoughton.

Hancock, R., Smith, P., Sheath, G. and Beetlestone, F. (1994) Getting started on the PICC project, in H. Dombey and M. Meek (eds) *First Steps Together*. Stoke on Trent: Trentham Books.

Hanna, G. (1996) A bunch of fives sorts out the boys, *Times Educational Supplement*, 19 April 1996: 21.

Harlen, W. (1992) *The Teaching of Science*. London: David Fulton.

Hazareesingh, S. (1991) *The Poverty of a Pedagogy: A Holistic View of the National Curriculum in the Early Years*. London: Building Blocks Occasional Paper No. 1. London: Building Blocks Educational.

Hudson, L. (1966) *Contrary Imaginations*. Harmondsworth: Penguin.

Hudson, L. (1968) *Frames of Mind*. Harmondsworth: Penguin.

Hudson, L. (1970) The question of creativity, in P.E. Vernon (ed.) *Creativity*. Harmondsworth: Penguin.

Hughes, M. (1981) Can pre-school children add and subtract?, *Education Psychology*, 3: 207–19.

Hughes, P. (1991) *Gender Issues*. Leamington Spa: Scholastic.

Hurst, V. (1994) The implications of the national curriculum for nursery education, in G.M. Blenkin and A.V. Kelly (eds) *The National Curriculum and Early Learning: An Evaluation*. London: Paul Chapman.

King, R. (1978) *All Things Bright and Beautiful?* Chichester: John Wiley and Sons.

Kyriacou, C. (1986) *Effective Teaching in Schools*. Hemel Hempstead: Simon and Schuster.

Kyriacou, C. (1991) *Essential Teaching Skills*. Hemel Hempstead: Simon and Schuster.

Lancaster, J. (ed.) (1987) *Art, Craft and Design in the Primary School*. Corsham: NSEAD.

Lewis, A. (1991) *Primary Special Needs and the National Curriculum*. London: Routledge.

Lipman, M. (1991) *Thinking in Education*. Cambridge: Cambridge University Press.

Lowenfeld, V. and Lambert Brittain, W. (1982) *Creative and Mental Growth*, 7th edition. London: Collier Macmillan.

Mallon, B. (1989) *Children Dreaming*. Harmondsworth: Penguin.

Maslow, A. (1954) *Motivation and Personality*. New York: Harper and Row.

McNamara, S. (1995) Let's cooperate – developing children's social skills in the classroom, in J. Moyles (ed.) *Beginning Teaching, Beginning Learning*. Buckingham: Open University Press.

McKinnon, D.W. (1962) The personality correlates of creativity: a study of American architects, in P.E. Vernon (ed.) *Creativity*. Harmondsworth: Penguin.

Meade, A. and Cubey, P. (1995) *Thinking Children*. Wellington: New Zealand Council for Educational Research with the Institute for Early Childhood Studies.

Measor, L. and Sikes, P. (1992) *Gender and School*. London: Cassell.

Mednick, S.A. (1962) The associative basis for the creative process, *Psychological Review*, 69: 220–32.

Merry, R. (1997) *Successful Children: Successful Teaching*. Buckingham: Open University Press.

Mertens, R. and Newland, A. (1996) Home works: shared maths and shared writing, in J. Bastiani and S. Wolfendale (eds) *Home–School Work in Britain*. London: David Fulton.

Miller, L. (1992) *Understanding your 4 year old*. London: Rosendale Press.

Milner, D. (1983) *Children and Race – 10 Years on*. Stroud: Alan Sutton.

Mosley, J. (1993) *Turn Your School Around*. Wisbech: LDA.

Mosley, J. (1996) *Quality Circle Time in the Primary Classroom*. Wisbech: LDA.

Moss, P. and Penn, H. (1996) *Transforming Nursery Education*. London: Paul Chapman.

Moyles, J. (1989) *Just Playing? The Role and Status of Play in Early Childhood Education*. Buckingham: Open University Press.

Moyles, J. (1992) *Organizing for Learning in the Primary Classroom*. Buckingham: Open University Press.

Moyles, J. (ed.) (1995) *Beginning Teaching: Beginning Learning in Primary Education*. Buckingham: Open University Press.

Moyles, J. and Suschitzky, W. (1997) *Jills of All Trades? Classroom Assistants in KS1 Classrooms*. London: ATL.

National Council for Educational Technology (1992) *Starting from Stories*. Coventry: NCET.

National Curriculum Council (1990a) *Curriculum Guidance 4: Education for Economic and Industrial Understanding*. York: NCC.

National Curriculum Council (1990b) *Curriculum Guidance 5: Health*. York: NCC.

National Curriculum Council (1990c) *Curriculum Guidance 7: Environmental Education*. York: NCC.

National Curriculum Council (1990d) *Curriculum Guidance 8: Citizenship*. York: NCC.

Newman, J.M. (1985) *Whole Language Theory in Use*. London: Heinemann.

Office for Standards in Education (1993a) *Well Managed Classes in Primary Schools: Case Studies of 6 Teachers*. London: HMSO.

Office for Standards in Education (1993b) *Curriculum Organisation and Classroom Practice in Primary Schools.* London: HMSO.

Office for Standards in Education (1993c) *Access and Achievement in Urban Education.* London: HMSO.

Office for Standards in Education (1993d) *The New Teacher in School.* London: HMSO.

Office for Standards in Education (1995) *Guidance on the Inspection of Nursery and Primary Schools.* Ofsted Handbook. London: HMSO.

Palmer, J. and Pettitt, D. (1993) *Topic Work in the Early Years.* London: Routledge.

Parnes, S.J. (1985) *A Facilitating Kind of Leadership.* Buffalo, NY: Bearly.

Peiffer, V. (1996) in M. Seaton, 'Portrait of the artist as a tortured soul', *The Independent on Sunday,* 7 April 1996.

Piaget, J. (1973) *The Child's Conception of the World.* St. Albans: Granada.

Piotrowski, J. (1996) *Expressive Arts in the Primary School.* London: Cassell.

Pluckrose, H. (1993) *Starting School – The Vital Years.* Hemel Hempstead: Simon and Schuster.

Race Relations Act (1976) London: HMSO.

Read, H. (1943) *Education Through Art.* London: Faber.

Rist, R. (1970) Student social class and teacher expectations: the self fulfilling prophesy in ghetto education, *Harvard Educational Review,* 40(3): 411–51.

Robinson, G. (1989) Stimulus for art in the primary school: an historical perspective, in A. Dyson (ed.) *Looking, Making and Learning.* London: Institute of Education and Kogan Page.

Robson, S. and Smedley, S. (1996) *Education in Early Childhood.* London: David Fulton.

Ross, A., Hutchings, M., Craft, A. and Mottocks, B. (1990) *The Primary Enterprise Pack.* London: PNL Press.

Ross, R. and Browne, N. (1993) *Girls as Constructors in the Early Years.* Stoke on Trent: Trentham Books.

Rothenstein, M. (1986) *Michael Rothenstein: Drawings and Paintings aged 4–7 1912–1917.* London: Redstone Press (pages unnumbered).

Rowe, D. and Newton, J. (1994) *You, Me, Us.* London: Citizenship Foundation.

Runnymede Trust (1993) *Equality Assurance in Schools, Quality, Identity, Society.* London: Trentham Books.

Ryle, G. (1949) *Concept of Mind.* London: Hutchinson.

Sex Discrimination Act (1975) London: HMSO.

Shallcross, D. (1981) *Teaching Creative Behaviour.* Buffalo, NY: Prentice Hall.

Sherwin, J. (1990) The use of construction kits to foster equal opportunity, CDT, and collaborative learning, in E. Tutchell (ed.) *Dolls and Dungarees.* Buckingham: Open University Press.

Sisk, D. (1981) Foreword in D. Shallcross *Teaching Creative Behaviour*. Buffalo, NY: Prentice Hall.

Skinner, D. (1996) Unpublished interview notes.

Straker, A. (1985) Positive steps, *Times Educational Supplement*, 5 April 1985.

Suffolk County Council (1985) *Art in the First Years of Schooling 4–11*. Suffolk: Berol.

Sylvester, R. (1991) *Start with a Story*. Birmingham: Development Education Centre.

Taylor, R. and Andrews, G. (1993) *The Arts in the Primary School*. London: The Falmer Press.

Temple, C., Nathan, R., Temple, F. and Burris, N.A. (1988) *The Beginnings of Writing*. London: Allyn and Bacon.

Tizard, B., Blatchford, P., Burke, J., Farquhar, C. and Plewis, I. (1988) *Young Children at School in the Inner City*. Hove: Lawrence Erlbaum Associates.

Torrance, E.P. (1962) *Guiding Creative Talent*. Englewood Cliffs, NJ: Prentice Hall.

Torrance, E.P. (1963) *Education and The Creative Potential*. London: Oxford University Press.

Vygotsky, L.S. (1978) *Mind in Society: The Development of Higher Psychological Processes*. Cambridge, MA: MIT Press.

Walden, R. and Walkerdine, V. (1982) *Girls and Mathematics from Primary to Secondary Schooling*. Bedford Way Papers No. 24. London: Institute of Education.

Warnock, M. (1976) *Imagination*. London: Faber and Faber.

Wheatley, D. (1992) Environmental education – an instrument of change?, in G. Hall (ed.) *Themes and Dimensions of the National Curriculum*. London: Kogan Page.

Whyte, J. (1986) *Girls into Science and Technology (GIST)*. London: Routledge and Kegan Paul.

Willig, C. J. (1990) *Children's Concepts and the Primary Curriculum*. London: Paul Chapman.

Wolfendale, S. (1992) *Empowering Parents and Teachers*. London: Cassell.

Wood, D. (1988) *How Children Think and Learn*. Oxford: Basil Blackwell.

Wood, E. and Attfield, J. (1996) *Play, Learning and the Early Childhood Curriculum*. London: Paul Chapman.

Woods, P. (1995) *Creative Teachers in Primary Schools*. Buckingham: Open University Press.

Yardley, A. (1970) *Senses and Sensitivity*. London: Evans Brothers.

Young, J.G. (1982) Negative spaces, *Journal of Creative Behaviour*, 16(4): 256–64.

Index